WILLIAM NEILL is a prolific poet
Places, Making Tracks and *Four*
Ayrshire in 1922 and grew up sp
language of the heart'. He is well known for his fierce pride in the three
languages of his poetry, English, Scots and Gaelic, and his commentary
on Scottish life and culture. In 1969 he won the Bardic Crown at the
National Gaelic Mod in Aviemore, a great achievement as he did not
learn Gaelic until he was an adult. In 1984 he received a grant from the
Scottish Arts Council which helped him become a full-time writer.

Neill spent 30 years serving in the RAF as a fitter and navigator. On
leaving he enrolled as a mature student at Edinburgh University, gradu-
ating in 1971 with a degree in Celtic Studies. Following this he spent 10
years teaching English in Galloway. Neill has travelled widely and trans-
lated various works from classical and modern languages. He has had
many articles published in literary magazines, including *Lallans* of which
he was once editor. He now lives in Castle Douglas.

Caledonian Cramboclink

Verse, broadsheets and in conversation

WILLIAM NEILL

Luath Press Limited

EDINBURGH

www.luath.co.uk

First published 2001

The paper used in this book is neutral-sized and recyclable.
It is made in Scotland from elemental chlorine free
pulps sourced from renewable forests.

'On Satire, Mavericks and Scotland: William Neill in conversation with
Gerry Cambridge' is reproduced by kind permission of *The Dark Horse*, the
Scottish-American poetry magazine edited by Gerry Cambridge.

The publisher acknowledges subsidy from

THE SCOTTISH ARTS COUNCIL

towards the publication of this volume

Printed and bound by
IBT Global, London and New York

Typeset in 10.5 point Sabon by
S. Fairgrieve and A. Drews, Edinburgh

Contents

CONTENTS

Foreword

WILLIAM NEILL CALLS this book of poems *Cramboclink* and defines the word as 'doggerel' or rhyming verse. One would hardly call these poems 'doggerel'. But Neill certainly writes for the most part in rhyming verse. And indeed having himself been attacked for writing in rhyme, he fights back by saying that for the most part modern poetry is spiritless and over-delicate. One could never accuse Neill of being that.

His poetry is robust and opinionated in the best sense and much of it is satirical. He has targets which he aims for and often hits. He is a strong Scottish patriot and finds it hard to disguise his loathing of 'panloaf' or RP speech and the loss of so many wonderful Scots words. In a poem called the 'Scotlit Cringe' he writes:

> Yon Scottish blauds will haurdlie airn a fee
> gin ye're no yin a *London* critic picks.

He ends the poem with the words:

> Luik southarts gin ye'd be a bard-o-pairts.

Not only is this true of the poet, he says, it is also very obviously true of the politician. And one must admit that there is a certain truth in this, that there has been in Scotland a feeling that one must please a cosmopolitan London. On the other hand how can one appease London if one writes in Scots. MacDiarmid himself was never wholly accepted there or given his due as a poet of genius. Thus of course writing in Scots is a political as well as aesthetic gesture. In any case Neill calls Scots the language of the heart, that is to say, it was the language he grew up on in Ayrshire. Furthermore, Neill is a scholar as well as a poet. He knows his Latin and his Greek and his Italian and he points us to other languages in the same position as Scots. Dante himself wrote in Florentine and deserted Latin.

It is possible that it is this robustness that critics of modern poetry find themselves uncomfortable with. There are so many Hamlets about that to find a brisk Fortinbras who knows what he thinks and says what he means is strange to them. Neill can be ironical when he wants as when he points to a laird's retinue at the Highland Games as being exactly like sheep, a simile which calls up a brilliant historical judgement, for the laird of course put out his tenants in order to make way for sheep.

Neill castigates those figures who array themselves in the trappings of false Scottishness. To them Burns is the only poet who ever lived.

> Adapt! adapt! fashion's for Mawket Fawces
> point your nose southwards, where the boys done
>   well,
> rhyme 'law' with 'poor' and tell your Secketary
> to Sloane it proply so that those Paw Cheps
> in Indiar, Africar, Australiar and Americar
> know where the loom of language spins its
>   thread....

There is no doubt that Neill is enraged by what he sees as the thinness of modern English and by the way in which deviation from it is considered as barbaric. He is a fierce defender of the variety of languages and writes:

> How many of the language purists know
> that pylgeint comes from pulicantio
> Roman reveille, soldiers' sparrow-fart,
> Old Taffy's dagreu are Homer's dakrua:
> Tears, idle tears, and some know what they mean –
> I dash my staff in wrath upon the ground
> at August Twelfth birdshots in philabegs
> who do not know Buachaill is Boukolos.

This is the genuine voice of the outraged scholar: and there is little doubt that again he is right, that there is prejudice against for example, Scots and Welsh in favour of a central RP, and that this in turn reflects a political imperialism.

Neill himself writes in three languages; English, Scots and Gaelic. Gaelic he learnt for its authenticity and has made himself fluent in the language. He has some fine translations in this book of Gaelic poems and of course he has original Gaelic poems of his own. He says a very perceptive thing about Duncan Ban Macintyre who, after he left Ben Dorain, went to Edinburgh where his wonderful gift for imaginatively natural description deserted him:

> Fair Duncan of the songs
> Grey Duncan of the doggerel
> the fate of all bards
> when time takes the hill from them

He has a very funny translation of a Catullus poem and one of a Verlaine poem.

Neill is a very talented exponent of rhymed verse as one can see from the following:

> The Honourable Hermione Chummleigh-
>   Bummleigh
> was wed this morning in St Chasuble's
> in virgin white and all the family valuables
> under old Norman pillars, quaint and crumbly.
> The forelock-touchers view the splendour humbly:
> old Chummleigh-Bummleigh thought it scarcely
>   passable.
> Portly, port-winey and irascible,
> thought of The Abbey foiled and fuming dumbly.

It is no writer of doggerel who can create these ingenious rhymes, and often Neill sets himself difficult ones.

Neill seems to me a classicist who regrets the decline of the classical world into vulgarity. He is also however someone who applauds Dante for writing in Florentine, not in Latin. He attacks pseuds of all kinds, especially Scottish pseuds who have gone over to the 'other side' and deserted their own language and people. He is a flayer of the artificial and the hypocritical. He is a poet and scholar with very strong opinions. He is a very funny satirist, shrewd and honest, with an eye and an ear for the corrupt. He is a good warrior in the service of his beliefs. may he long continue to write.

Iain Crichton Smith

Preface

MY WORK IN THE GAELIC MAGAZINE *Gairm* and *Lallans*, the magazine for writing in Scots, shows that I could equally well have written this preface in those more indigenous tongues. That I choose to do so in English is simply because it is known to a larger readership. This collection is written in all three tongues with ample glosses and translations for the benefit of all who are less acquainted with Gaelic and Scots than with English.

During my days in Edinburgh I noticed a street named Thornie Bauk, and nearby another called Drumdryan Street. The first name is Scots, the other Gaelic. Both refer to the strip of land used in the runrig system of agriculture to separate one strip or holding of land from the other, an unploughed section on which a rough thorn hedge grew. Scotland is an old and embattled nation. It has quite recently been mocked, both on the air and in London newspapers, as being a place barbaric and without culture. The work of Robert Burns was described by one London scribbler as gibberish. When such hacks are assailed by indignant Scots we usually receive the suave reply that we should develop a sense of humour. Here and there in this collection, I answer such jibes, and offer any objector to them same response as we receive from London.

As for *Cramboclink*, this word is sometimes defined as 'doggerel', sometimes as 'rhyming verse'. The latter definition, if not the more accurate, is certainly the kinder. Since I have always believed that alleged verse (even free verse) should have a recognisable rhythm I have now and then been the target of those who prefer the 'essence-distillers of fine verse'. At worst I have been called a 'cramboclinker' and occasionally 'a mere competent versifier'. I object to the qualifying 'mere' but certainly not to the rest of that title, since most poets until today have been competent versifiers: Homer, Shakespeare, Robert Burns and many others.

There is a school of poets who seem to have the view that 'true poems' should resemble a mystical incantation. There is a kind of poetry which may deserve such a title. But our ancestors used verse for many purposes: satire, narrative, elegy and humour to name but a few.

I write a great deal in Scots, for that is the language of the heart, and I remember it as it was spoken by the miners and farm workers in my native Ayrshire. It is a very Scottish place indeed which gave birth to Coel Hen, William Wallace, Robert Bruce, Walter Kennedy, Alexander Montgomerie, and Robert Burns. It was an area in which Welsh gave way in turn to Gaelic and Scots. Walter Kennedy and Alexander Montgomerie were speakers of Ayrshire Gaelic. Unfortunately the process of anglicisation has deprived the people of Scotland of such knowledge. I can trace my ancestry by record in that airt back at least to the sixteenth century and may assume that some of my forebears were there before that date. If my genes were not in some way affected by the tongues they spoke, my spirit certainly is.

As to my verse in Gaelic, though the southwest was once regarded (as recent scholarship shows) as being as 'heilant' as any place north of the Forth-Clyde line I was obliged to obtain a share in the old tongue pestering native speakers, and to enhance my knowledge of it by a course in the University of Edinburgh which embraced all the island's Celtic tongues. I do not claim to be a well-qualified academic, but I did get a middling honours degree and subsequently sat in the classes of that fine man 'Jake' MacDonald of Jordanhill. All his lectures and lessons were in Gaelic.

William Neill
April 2001

For Doctor George Philp*

I heard a chiel yince cry ye Doctor Rigbane,
he tellt me hou ye'd caa't his spondyls back
intil thair ain richt bit. Whit care ye'd tak
ti pit his sair nesh banes ti wark again
Man, Geordie, it's a ferlie hou ye hain
the blauds o bards an scrievers. Ye maun lack
eftir yir lang sair daurg wi banes that crack
yae meinit o the day ti cry yir ain

Weill, in yae wey the twa daurgs are the same:
speirits an hairts can hae thair fankils tae
an want a skeilie haund ti sort thair knots.

Ye wad bring native bards an sauls ti fame
in this puir laund that's gey near tint the wey
ti mak mair stieve the rigbane o the Scots.

---

* George Philp graduated M.B. Ch.B. from Edinburgh in 1955 and from the London
College of Osteopathy in 1961 and found time from his medical practice to record
in sound and vision the work of Scottish poets and writers under the SCOTSOUN
and SCOTSEEN impresses.

Guid Speik

(Frae the Milanese o the makkar Carlo Porta, 1775-1821, on being tellt no ti mak duans in that tung)

The wards o a language Maister Brawspeik Sir
are like a wee palette o monie hues,
the warst or bonniest picter ye micht chuse
hings on the penter's maisterie an virr.

Athoot some mense, guid thocht an character
ti redd the wards o onie guid discoorse
the tungs o aa the warld wad hae nae force
abune the trash o onie haverin cletterer.

An aa guid nories, mainners that ye ken
are no in the kist o onie single speik,
but in thir harns that hae the tung's richt threid.

Yon's true ither in the mooth o learit men,
yaisin the maist apruvit panloaf-leid,
or onie tung that ye micht wiss wes deid.

The first four lines of Porta's sonnet read:

I paroll d'on lenguagg, car sur Gorell,
hin ona tavolozza de color,
che ponn fà el quader brutt, e el ponn fa bell
segond la maestria del pittor.

As compared to *official* Italian

Le parole di una lingua, caro signor Gorelli
sona uno tavolozza di colori,
che pono rendere il quadro brutto, e lo possono
rendere bello
a seconda della maestria del pittore.

Derval*

Yellow-haired Derval of Galloway
sitting in the corner of my vision,
I do not care that you were the mother of lords
or a friend of heroes,
cherished by the lion of Loch Awe.

But that you were from this place
before the loss of our heritage
fostering poetry and song.

But now in your native woods
who that has ears to hear
could put words to those airs?

Yellow-haired Derval of Galloway
I hear your voice again
faintly across the years,
in a poem of past time,
when they knew you
in Galloway of the green glens.

---

* In *The Book of the Dean of Lismore* W J Watson's note states that Derval (Dear-
Bhail) was from Gallaibh, 'The Lowlands' or Galloway. The name Dearbhal is pos-
sibly a variant of Devorgilla (a Galloway name) and I took it as such. In those days
(15c) there was little cultural or linguistic difference between SW Scotland and the
Highlands, viz. *The Flyting of Dunbar and Kennedy.*

Bobbie, Zzyne an Aa That

Wha kens Rab Burns that's never driven gyte
wi *Robbie, Bobbie, Zzyne* insteid o *sss-yne*;

ti ken that Scots hes *dicht*, an niver *dight*
an aye a 'ready *slicht*' insteid o *slight*
What tho on hamely haggis we may dine
washed doun wi usquebae or yill or wine
wha isna scunnert wi a murdert line?

I ken thare's no ower monie o us left
that kens a *bullock* here is aye a *stot*
an ken a dyke's a *waa* an no a *watter*.

But aye some nyaff o tung and harns bereft
or some great figure o the 'meeja' lot
will fankle RABBIE'S line wi fremit patter.

Daft Rabbie

I mynd him yet, his roon, reid sonsie face
big smilin mou, teeth lik a dyke wi slaps
the braw, plain, thick tweed suit, big buits
med clean and trig bi his auld weeda mither
Ten years gied me mair harns nor his twa-score

Nou thay wad cry him *mentally disadvantaged*
in thae days thay jist kirsent him plain *daft,*
eleiven ti the dizzen. Staundin in the dure
o the fairm kitchen, a muckle skep on's airm
bringin the weemin's orders up the brae
an howpin ti be bidden ti his denner
thare wi the men. Thay wad speir at him
an lauch at his repone. He didna tak
the strunts at aa thair coorslik taislin.

But lat him chaise a penny or a shillin
ti see gin he wad tak the bigger yin –
he wesna jist *that* daft
Yae day a traiveller tried him oot wi paper
an laucht the ither side o's sleikit face
when Rabbie stecht it in his waiskit-pooch.

A richt ferlie whan he dee'd. Ye wad hae thocht
it wes the provost. The kirk lipper-fu
the kirkyaird fairlie hotchin. The haill bit
turnt oot in murnin-claes.

Dafties wes scant o hairns, no sowls;
had ti be yirdit lik mair mensefu bodies.

We're kinder nouadays. We dinna cry thaim daft.
and dinna chaise ti lauch at whit thay say.

Marching the Wall

More of a scribbler than soldier, not much fun
marching behind a decurion on the Wall
keeping the pax for those who want to run
this sodden isle if ever Rome should fall.
Between two tribes we walk, tame in the South,
aping our ways and happy beneath the forts,
raging and wild in the north, but they're all mouth,
though they need watching. Spies in their savage courts
tell of their drinking and boasting and rebel songs;
impudent bards who mock the Latin measure
with parody in their own barbaric tongues,
vying to give their gilded chieftains pleasure.
It's many a mile from this knuckle-end to Rome
and further still to Tarentum, sunny home.

They say if I keep marching long enough
I'll get a bag of coin and a rustic patch
that's all my own, although unploughed and rough,
if I'm not seen off in some border stabbing match.
Marcus, time served, with phalerae a-clinking,
dreams of a Gaulish farm; scores off each day:
walks on the safer side and he's stopped drinking
posca to cheer him up. Who knows some stray
stone from a clansman seeking tribal glory
won't get him yet for all his careful strappings,
to put an end to his long warrior story
and set us to casting lots to share his trappings.
When he tells of old battles, how Lollius commended him,
I wish that some barbarian lance had ended him.

A Bitter Note to Lord Byron

'There is no question at all about his rank as poet: he is not a poet but a writer of verses.' Kenneth Allott on Aldous Huxley.

I don't know if you're ash or dust or ghost,
Lord George, theology is so confusing.
I must assume your spirit moves at most
Somewhere in Hell or Limbo. Sex and boozing
Are said to qualify one to be lost
To better places. Beggers can't be choosing:
Mere versifiers as you know yourself
have even less of piety than pelf.

What's that, my Lord, or may I call you George –
You're bored to death with poets and their writings?
The limping odes that most of them disgorge,
The staggering sonnets and the bitter flytings,
The crossword-puzzle cryptograms they forge,
Rival reviews, score-settling backbitings-
I see your point, but spare me just a minute
To speak of my own day and poetry in it.

Mere versifiers – you won't like that mere –
I know you're fond of tropes like rhyme and metre,
That fill our modern critics with such fear –
Now verses hobble, stagger, limp and teeter
Upon the brink of bathos. These appear
Opaque to me, brought up on lyrics sweeter
Than those that decorate the magazines
much read in modern literary scenes.

I heard one rather unkind critic say
My own stuff wasn't made for modern times,
Might have gone down much better in your day,
Being like yourself an addict of strange rhymes.
Ottava rima simply does not pay:
As Ezra's Nixon said: dollars and dimes,
Come from the shelves under Romance or Mystery –
These have a more enduring fiscal history.

Alas, this critic said: 'Try aiming higher
Try to avoid the sort of stuff you write:
Those crambo-clinking verses don't inspire
Much trust in editorial circles. Slight
And insult's what you'll get, if not more dire
Strictures on metred rhyme; however bright,
Those landscape lyrics, rural lines on plovers
Won't get you bound in hard and glossy covers.'

But like cold mutton after venison:
Rhyme after free verse, once you get the taste
For making lines that scan, the Muse's benison
Depends upon a mood that's almost chaste –
In faithfulness to form whenever pen is on
Blank paper, when the inner light needs haste
To fill it with the latest inspiration-
(Revised in hope of sometime publication).

But just between ourselves, George, very few
In our own time can stitch a skilful stanza –
Quite out of fashion what you used to do.
The uncontrolled vers-libre extravaganza
Is what goes down today: the rhyming crew
Are thought of as the Muse's Sancho Panza
On Rosinante's back, riding behind
The windmill-tilters of the free-verse kind.

Poets who ape you, George, just don't get in
To Modern Verses or The Poetry Blatt,
Now that plain prosody's become a sin –
Byronic epics land back on the mat.
Prizes for Poetry you cannot win
If you insist on rhyming stuff like that.
Such as yourself, my Lord, are now thought merely
Crambo-clink versifiers, yours sincerely:

William Neill

Glasgow Irish*

It all depends on when your folks came over –
if with King Fergus then you'll be all right,
the Pict admixture makes you Scottish quite...
but from the Tattie Blight you can't recover.

Even if your lot are somewhere in the middle
between King Fergie and the British Raj,
you can't dodge flute and shamrock, cap and badge,
or play mere Scottish reels upon your fiddle.

Wear non-committal colours, say there is no God,
and preach no texts except the Left Book Club,
hot bigotry makes room in the right pub,
for Papist Atheist or Agnostic Prod.

Kentigern's salmon swallowed his gold ring,
and spewed it up beside the Dear Green Place –
a symbol for the Scoto-Irish race
whose hammers crashed on steel like anything.

The liveried buses roved in Orange and Green,
splendidly neutral through the city wards,
along the river, past the silent yards,
more fitting target for sectarian spleen.

* The original *Scoti* were an Irish tribe brought over by Fergus MacErc. After the
  Reformation some went back, in the Plantation of Ulster. More Irish came to
  Scotland after the potato blight and famine in Ireland. Glasgow buses were painted
  orange and green. Marvellous what religion has done for the Scoto-Irish race! The
  great Hugh MacDiarmid on being asked what effect the Irish in Scotland would
  have on Scottish political aspirations, asked which Irish invasion the interviewer
  was referring to, adding that he approved of both.

Mull Ferry

O fair young Mairead, love has wounded me,
O fair young lass with eyes as dark as sloes...

We should have booked much earlier:
the car deck's absolutely packed.

The silver salmon I would take for you,
rich venison upon the hills of Mull...

The scenery's marvellous, all those hills and things.
But the people – a depressing lot.

Eyes clear as dewdrops hanging from the branch,
so blue and still in the early morn...

The important things, of course
are run by people like ourselves.

O fair young Mairead, were I only there
in the high mountains of Mull with you...

Home Thoughts in the Piazza

We were remote and running on scythed wheels
when these were polished, regular, urbane,
between the *altopiano* and the plain
where Dante's compeers rigged their daggered schemes.

Sweet-sounding strings, under an evening sky
smooth as shot silk above the colonnade;
where mercenaries marched and Ceasar played,
we sit and sip within a warm wind's sigh.

On our wet moorland by their last frontier,
brown water roars to white through scattered stone;
this, our first sculpture, carved by time alone,
stubbornly in our vision, even here.

Faurweill ti Yestereen

*(Frae the Gaelic o Niall Mòr MacMhuirich, c.*1600*)*

A lang faurweill ti yesternicht
a sharrow stang nou that it's gane
gif I sud thole the widdie's heicht
yet wad I lieve it ower again.

Twa thare are ben this hoose the nicht
wha canna smoor the ee's bricht wiss
nor dern awa frae ither's sicht
a glisk o luve as fain's a kiss.

The glisks o luve that flicht atween
As shair as onie kiss maun seal
the saicret memorie o yestereen
the waesome stoun o hairt's faurweill

The clashin tongue in vain may seek
oor sang o luve, o bonnie een
that seek mine frae the chaumer neuk
an tell yince mair my ain hairt's een.

O that the nicht wad never gae,
was never come the dawin bricht
sae we sud be thegither aye,
Arise ma hairt, an smoor the licht.

Summer Coast Road, Ballantrae

Once, said my father, scarce a body came
along this road. Sometimes a pony and trap
would meet another and the drivers swap
a word between the market-place and home.

Now nose to tail along the crowded shore,
they weave and dodge and risk their necks to pass
between the hillside and the marram grass.
No sound but blasting horn and engine's roar.

Dad's time was slow: now you can fairly fly
past this whole rocky coastline in a day,
eyes on the road, no longer need to stay
and idle by the verge with passers-by.

Dundrennan

Here was a queen's last rest before the ferry
took her to exile in the final prison;
far from the iron kirk she sought to bury
too many sins beneath an English heaven.

Unhappy widowed and unhappy wed,
south to scant mercy made her pilgrimage
from a rough country to a rougher bed,
intrigue and counter and the axe's edge.

While time and prejudice knocked down the walls,
burned the poor land to fuel Genevan fires,
turned to another purpose choir and stalls
and used the scattered stone to build new byres.

Greek Island

When new-born rosy-fingered dawn arose,
a silence reigned throughout the high hotel.
I walked from the room to look on the wine-dark bay.

Here from the lofty balcony I saw
long lines of empty sunbeds by the shore
where the white maggots of the west would warm
to brown chrysalis shapes in the high sun.

In the old town, Levantine merchants stirred
waiting for the slap of sandals on the cobbles
around the ruined mosques, deserted libraries,
alien theologies set in a different script.
The Turks have given way to Frankish feet.

A towel stakes a claim by the lapping sea
that flows from Troy to the Pillars of Hercules;
lost now the golden apples of the sun
stolen from the dread gods by later thieves.

On the acropolis, Ionic columns frame
views of the new colossus, square, concrete
stretching as far as the modern eye can see.

God Said ti Me

(Paul Verlaine, 1844-1896)

God said ti me: 'Ma suin, ye maun loe me,
ma dirkit side; ma hairt that bleeds an shines,
ma wundit feet that Magdalen has sined,
ma airms raxt oot sae sairlie on the tree,
wi aa yir sins. An ma haunds! See this gallows tae,
the nails, the gaw, the spoonge and aa the mairks –
sae loe nocht else amang the fause warld's warks
but ma Flesh, ma Bluid an the Ward I say

Hae I no loed ye until daith itsel,
bairns o yae Faither, ma sune in the Spreit –
did I no thole for ye this wierdit thing?

Yir sairest stangs, hae I no bled ti stell,
hae I no swat amang yir nichtlie sweit?
Puir freen, wha hunts for me whaur here I hing?'

Mynd Whit Barrie Said*

In Scotland ye'll no get yir nits
till yir teeth's ower foondert ti crack thaim
Whan yir banes are aa skailt roun in bits
thay bigg mausoleums ti back thaim.**

It's the yae orra bit that I ken
whaur withoot yae syllab o the leid,
ye can write o the bardrie o men
jist as shuin as they're daicentlie *deid*.

Dinae bother ye're jimp o the wards
for yon isna onie gret maitter,
gin ye ken but the *name* o the bards
yir review ma weill publiss the better.

Tae sclimm til the uttermaist peak
o whit passes nou for Parnassus,
jist get yirsel thirled ti a clique
an they'll see that yir cramboclink passes

Dinna think that they're lukkin for skeil,
or mind onie haet whit ye're screivin...
plain havers will dae jist as weill
aboot auld duans weill bye beleivin.

But mynd, thare's yae thing ye maun ken,
haud this shenackle firm in yir heid
that gin ye're kenspeckle wi men,
ye micht no be weill-kent when ye're deid.

---

* In Scotland you don't get your nuts until you have no teeth left to crack them.
  Attributed to J M Barrie.

** Remember Burns.

Eftir the Yirdin

Socrates said: It's aither dwaumless sleep
eftir ye're deid or it's a better crack
ye's get frae aa yon bauld Homeric pack
not onie orra blethers, sae drink deep
o Daith's fell quaich, for whae wad want ti keep
his buits aye paidlin in this mortal glaur
when later conversation's better faur
an turns doun yirdlie gabbin ti a peep?

Yon gies a bodie mair encouragement
nor Tally Dante's dowie kirkyaird verse
ten-laftit Paradise an nine-fauld Hell.

Till ye refleck naebodie kent
whit isn't that follies on frae kist and hairse.
Bleck naething, clarsachs, raistin, wha can tell?

Holy Wedlock*

The Honourable Hermione Chummleigh-Bummleigh
was wed this moring in St Chasuble's
in virgin white and all the family valuables,
under old Norman pillars, quaint and crumbly.
The forelock-touchers viewed the splendour humbly:
old Chummleigh-Bummleigh thought it scarcely passable.
Portly, port-winey and irascible,
thought of The Abbey, foiled and fuming dumbly.

Crossed swords and sashes; bridegroom a rare swell,
a lord, no ten-a-penny hunting squire.
Their children will be Honourables too.

They say her Daddy was obliged to sell
a thousand acres, Badger's Wood entire
to settle what came free to quite a few.

* After perusing a 'society' magazine in a dentist's waiting room.

Elegy

Betrayed by sentiment I wander back
across damp grass to read the names and dates,
late in the day grown conscious of a lack
of due respect for old certificates:
childbirth and matrimony, black-edged death
lapsed milestones, thought important in their day:
faded brown letters, history's ghostly breath,
daguerrotypes my father stowed away
saying: 'Old rubbish cluttering up the place –
anyway, past your grandad and grandmother
they're nameless members of the human race;
one silly smirk is very like another –
and not a single one of them a gent
or dame for all their earrings and fake pearls,
half-hunters, alberts and dundrearies meant
to make them look important. None were earls.'
Just to make sure I checked them all myself:
joiners and slaters, publicans and sinners –
one tinker even. Very little wealth
and scarcely one of what we now call 'winners'.
Here a last notice over narrow lairs
limns out their final resting-place on stone
marking for those who brood on such affairs
how mind and muscle soon desert the bone.
There's not a single one who was cremated
purposely. (Bones could stand on Judgement Day).
They lie with shuffling-off times neatly dated
except for those wrapped up in alien clay,
whose bones received to family dispensation
soldiers and sailors passing with a curse
for King-Queen-Politics-and-Nation
dying of punctured hides or something worse.

Flanders, Gallopoli, Zulu, Boer, Crimea –
uniformed peasants dodging native earth,
not in pursuit of any great idea,
or fighting for their Dear Old Native Earth –
but tired to death, like me of humdrum toiling
for gaffer's gain in factory or byre,
from all these descent honest jobs recoiling
to jump from frying pan into the fire.

What atavistic yearning brought me here
to mope on names and dates and mouldering bones
among the fallen leaves, the dying year,
the tumbled flower-vases, serried stones?
But that these forebears from whence life has fled
mean more than sociologists discuss:
what random choice made these assorted dead
base for the apex ending up with *us*?

Deodorant Advert

(Catullus, LXIX)

Don't you know Rufus, why those lovely creatures
won't let you bed 'em for those gifts laid out
of diamonds, dresses, jewels – things that feature
much in your wooings? There's a tale about
that says your armpits have a horrid pong
like something dead and that's what makes 'em scared.
There's no good-looking bird will come along
to get her nose filled when your armpit's bared –
so get some stuff to chase that stink today
or pretty darlings just won't come your way

and in Scots......

Deodorant Advert

(Catullus, 87-54 BC, Latin)

Weill, Roy ma laddie, hou can ye no see
nae bonnie lass will ligg aside yir thie,
for gifts o silken claith an glentin stanes
while yon reek frae yir oxters aye remains?
It stangs yir hairt, ye say, yon nestie tale
that says a gait wad hae a sweeter smell.
Gin oor nebs runkle at yer stink's rebuff
whit douce wee thing can thole yir manky guff?
Sine oot yon ugsome yowder eidentlie
or dinnae wunner hou the weemin flee

Poem LXIX

37

Drumcraigie

They call the place Drumcraigie, rocky ridge,
a clinty outcrop justifies the name –
three syllables that hold a Gaelic edge;
through the long centuries it stayed the same.
Well. What's the odds? Only a fool would care
to labour points about a vanished tongue
that set its style upon the hilltop there,
when an old tribe was vigorous and young.
Yet there are some won't let the byname go
into some newer speech as if they'd hold
for all forgetting, to a feebler glow
of ancient things remembered, storied gold
lost to the modern and more useful sense,
mind's armour for this new indifference.

Kailyaird Duan

The hoggets hiddle in the howe
the rain comes dingin doun,
I courie doun ablo the knowe,
an hap ma coatie roun.

I'll bet ye'll cry this *crambo-clink*
an *kailyard verse* as weill,
wha gies a docken whit ye think?
the *facks* o it are *real*.

For watter daes tuim frae the lift
sheep courie doun forbye.
I'll get fair droukit gin I shift –
lat ithers mulk the kye.

Sae thinkna yir ain duans shine
for bletherin in RP
yir quittance daesna better mine
gin sheep are aa ma fee.

Caorann

Se bliadhna a nis bho chur mi caorann ann.
Uair eile 's bidh na dearcan ruadh air gheug
gan sgeadachadh le loinn deireadh an fhoghair.
Ach chaneil fhios ma bhios mi fhèin gam faicinn.

Leugan a chuireas aoibhneas air neacheigin,
is math gu faic fear-siubhal a mhaise ùr,
'se fuirich greis ag eisdeachd ris an tlàth-ghaoth
troimh mheangain luaisgeanach an uaigneas seo.

Rowan

It's a year now since I planted a rowan
Some other time red berries will be on the branch
decorating them with the last beauty of autumn,
but I don't know if I myself will see them.

Jewels that will give joy to someone else;
fine if some traveller sees their fresh grace,
and stands awhile to listen to the breeze
through waving branches in this lonely place.

Unkipling the Raj

*Ana zobbut Inglesi tiara;**
sweating after tiffin on his charpoy
MacCowal idly reads the yellow chit:
I am an English flying officer,
take me to the authorities and you will be well rewarded.

Being neither English nor an officer
within the meaning of the act,
but a half-pissed sergeant of the protectorate
he wonders why he is protecting
people who do not want to be protected,
neither by him,
nor by their mutual overlords.

On the veranda Abdul
contemplates the jebel
in the bright red distance.
There is surely but one God
*malik al youm endeen;***
perhaps tomorrow the shaweesh
will pay him the twenty piastres
for the clean floor, for the washing,
for his sufferance of the ignorant mangling
of the holy tongue of the Faithful.

* I am an English Flying Officer

** King of the Day of Judgement

Gaeltacht Incident

In Gaelic Ireland I met a man who said
'Fill up my glass and I will give to you
a fair exchange in a lovely word or two
made many years ago in a blind man's head.'

'tis the song that Raftery made for Mary Haynes
on a stormy Sunday when his heart arose
and he falling in love with her by Kiltartan Cross:
sure now and you'll have it in Raftery's very strains.'

Blind Raftery's gone to the house of Ballylee,
to the golden hair, to the red wine on the board –
If there should come all Ireland's poet horde,
their words could not encompass her grace to me.

A poor peasant with his *caipin* worn awry
in a smoky bar on a Connemara Street,
whose words came readily, measured and smoothly sweet
raising Blind Raftery to my inner eye.

Clashfairnie's Daunner

I come up here, gin its no ower wat,
ti streik ma shanks oot an ti fill ma ee
wi yon faur hills an watter; no jist that –
I listen til a voice that speiks ti me.

I dinnae ken whit kinna voice it is
or whae it is; that daesna muckle maitter –
nor can I aye mak oot whit is't it says,
but weill I ken its no lik orra paitter.

God? I misdoot that I wad be sae prood,
as mak sic claims. Mebbe the deil himsel;
Hornie in sleikit guise, fillin ma heid
wi thochts that caa the thowless doun ti hell.

I canna say. It micht be thir auld stanes
skailt aa about like lairstanes on this muir,
pit oot some kinna souch that steirs the banes
an harns o daft auld men that daunner here.

Binna for kirsnins, waddins, funerals –
I'm no like thaim that hing aboot the kirk,
or tak up awkin spaewife's falderals,
like some wee bairn that's frichtit in the mirk.

But fine I ken here in the forenicht's lown
thare's whiles I bide wi harns aa tuim an howe
an shair eneuch, thir whuspers gaither roun
an full me wi a kinna oorie lowe.

Thay mak me luik at aa that I've been tellt
bi better fowk nor me; whit ti believe
an whitna wey ti gae. Thay gey near fullt
ma boss harnpan wi things they cudna prieve.

43

Politicks that wad bring The Gowden Age,
and *Wars ti End Aa Wars* hes come an gane,
but puirtith's wi us yet an teirant's rage –
nae fouth o pleisure an nae lack o pain.

Thare's whiles I daunner in the muin's last glent
whiles in the daurkenin saft smirr o rain
thenkin on how ma days hae aa been tint
an whit I'd dae gin I micht stairt again.

A menseless dwaum. Staunin in dayset's licht
owre thraan an dour ti lippen nou ti ocht,
ma banes gey shooglie, sinnens no that ticht,
I ken that nae Repone in life is claucht

An gin yon Voice be haulie or the Deil,
up on the muir eftir ma lifetime's wark
I ken that ocht it says, it says as weill
as onie dominie or onie kirk.

Larach*

On Drumconnard now, only the curlew calls.
Sadly a body may stand on that high place
beside bare gable end and scattered walls
to think of old magic tales and a vanished grace.

Foolish, they say, are the praisers of time past:
a wise man turns his face and hails the new
but bricks of hucksters hall will turn to dust
while Drumconnard's ruin whispers to the few.

*   Larach (*Gael.*) a ruin or foundation

Fainne Or An Sron Muice

Chuala mise nach robh gnothach
aca an Glaschu nan Ealain
le rudan Ceilteich mar Gàidhlig
nuair a bha Ruaraidh ag iarraidh
cobhair a dh'fhoilsicheadh leabhar

far an d' fhuair Ceanntighearn 'fhàinne.
B'fhearrde iad fàinne eile
chan ann a caolan bradain
ach te chopair on dùnan
an sròn an ùmaidh a thuirt sin.

A Gold Ring in a Pig's Nose

I heard that Glasgow of the Arts
had no concern for a Celtic thing like Gaelic,
when Rory* asked them for help
in publishing a book
where St Mungo found his ring.
They would be the better of another ring
not in the guts of a salmon
but a copper one from the dunghill
in the nose of the clown who said this.

* The eminent poet scholar and editor Derick Thomson (Ruaraidh MacThomais) was refused a publication grant from the European City of Culture for the book *European Poetry in Gaelic* on the mysterious grounds that it was not sufficiently relevant to Glasgow.

Sunday Papers from the South

Here is our knuckle end, our Northern Fastness,
A snuff of the Metropolis arrives:
Exotic southern needs, and new *Brief Lives*,
A window on the life-style of our masters,
The Ascot fashions, the career disasters.
We drink their exploits with out heathen eyes
As they drink up champagne that supplies
Such wit as thrives upon their lusher pastures.

They tell us that our land is Much Improved
Old Useless Industry now cleared away.
Ironmasters gone, who made our lives so hard.

There's leisure now the Steel Mill's been removed
To read about their booming, brighter day.
Free gifts of Nuclear Waste for our back yard.

Informants

Eagerly reading the book of the Gaelic scholar
more learned in phonetics than myself,
we came at last to the informants
telling their tales to us beside the hearth.

I saw each blue peak arising
in memory on *Arann of the many stags**,
I recalled the brown stag on the high summit;
I heard of the man a long year dancing;
the corpse that lost fresh blood to the guilty hand,
the lusty Gowdie and the laird's women,
and blood among the nettles of Lochranza.

Old stories that no one would believe today
but not to be discounted in the gloom.
Bringing me in again to the very hearthstone
of the Arran folk and they conversing
in the kind houses of a vanished culture.

And I came again to the Fair in Shiskine.

* From a 12th century Gaelic poem

The Stane

(On the return o the stane reivit bi Edward Langshanks.)

Yon muckle aislar Langshanks took awa,
Gin it's the richt yin doun and back again,
An no some pauchilt orra chuckie stane,
Is ti be pitten in its richtfu haa
Gin reival touns can settle things ava.
Jist whaur ti bring yon ferlie objeck ben
Seivin centuars later, isna eith ti ken
Whit tour or pailace gets it eftir aa.

Whit fur, I ask masel, this sudden yeuk,
Ti gie back whit thay wadna gie afore?
Thay maun think Scots are aa saft in the heid

Wee Jockie Bell-the-cat syne baits his heuk
Ti fleitch auld Scotia thro the selsame door
Gies us the stane whan we hae speirt for bried.

Null Thar An Aiseig

Chaneil clàr-thìde ann, aiseag dol thairis,
nuair bhios luchd-turuis ann a' phaidheas
faradh as freagarraiche bhon t-sluagh a mhàin
a tha fo chomainn siubhail an là sin fhèin.

Faraidhean pàighte, cuan doilleir ann,
eadar a mhòrthir is an tràigh gun iarraidh,
lag fada thall air fàire, glan an dràsd,
an caladh sàbhailte, is leinn gu sìorraidh.

Ferry Crossing

There is no time-table, a ferry crossing
when there are travellers enough to pay
the suitable fare from only those people
who are obliged to travel on that day.

Fare paid, a dark sea running.
between the mainland and the unsought shore,
dimly aware on the horizon: now clear
the safe haven, ours for evermore.

Sneachd Air Astar

Chi mi an diugh air astar
fallain sneachd air Meall Liath.
Carson nach theirinn *Millyea*
ainm is motha Gallda?
Ged tha iomadh sloinneadh Gàidhlig
air muinntir dùthchasach an àite
rinn iomadh linn eadar-dhealachadh.
Am beannaichte mise no mallaichte
le tuilleadh 'sa chòir de lèirsinn?

Distant Snow

I see in the distance today,
a cloak of snow atop Meall Liath,
Why do I not sae Millyea,
the more Lowland name?
Though there is many a Gaelic name
on the natives of this district
many generations have caused a separation.
Am I blessed or cursed
with too much vision?

Oronsaidh

Nis, on a tha tràghadh ann, gabhaidh sinn ceum
null thar a' ghaineamh chaiteineach gu Oronsaidh.
Ri taobh na làraich sinn 'nar suidhe 'labhairt
mu linntean borba roimh ar sàmhchair.

Manaich a' cumail fàire air an fhairrge
'toirt taing do Dhia 'sa chuan ag èirigh àrd,
a' bacadh birlinn Lochlannach 'san onfhadh.
Na farspagan a' gairm. An do thraogh an tìde?

Oronsay

Now there's an ebb tide, we will take a walk
across the rippled sand to Oronsay.
Beside the ruin we will sit talking
of savage times before our peacefulness.

Monks keeping watch upon the ocean
giving thanks to God and the sea rising high,
keeping the Norseman's galley bayed by storm.
The black gulls crying. Is the tide ebbing?

A Soor Face et the Clan Gatherin

Eftir the Heilant Ball thay had lest nicht
Thay fell in yonner ablo Arthur's Seat
an mairched doun the haill length o Princes Street
Stoppit the buses et the traffic's hicht
The haill jing-bang in tartan, bonnie sicht,
a hunner-strang pipe-baund, man! whit a treat –
Twa dizzen drummers rettlin oot the beat
Thair siller dirkies skinklin in the licht.

Afore thaim aa thare, wi his chieftain's cromag
MacNeoni o MacNeoni led his clan,
his eagle-feather wabbing ower his ee.

Some teuchter thare girned that it turned his stomach
ti see sic *caoraich* mairch ahint the man
whase forbear drave the feck atour the sea.

Battlements

The other day again I left the car
went over damp flat holms to the wide river
to where the old tower stands upon its ait,
splitting the waters for a sure defence.
Yet power baffled steel and the wall fell.

A startled hare rose up before my feet;
a pheasant lumbered up into the mist.
There was no other there but the mailed ghosts
watchful along the gaping embrasures.

They inched the great gun up to the hills vantage
to pierce the massive wall. My lord, they say,
certain no cannon-shot could breach the stone
took his meal calmly in the wide room
till a flying shard cut off his lady's hand.

Old fanciful tales? The mortar mixed with blood,
the men hanged for example by the gate,
high privilege of castle, cothouse slavery,
fine silk over monster bodies, cruel arrogance,
the feuds of envy, greed, malicious pride.

Eyes watched me across time from battlements;
through the grey centuries the armour jingled.
I walked away from ghost imaginings
till safely out of bowshot, hearing the sentry mock:
What better now, in your own squalid day?

Doire A' Ghrianstad

Tha doire bheag air an druim
is tha mi cinnteach,
gu robh i an còmhnaidh ann.
Nuair thig grianstad a' geamhraidh
is cruinne ruadh a' tuiteam air cul chraobh
is caomh leam creidsinn
nach eil mi gu tur nam aonar
ach tha sùilean eile thar tìm
maille rium, is an aon tlachd aca
on is e sin an là as giorra
is roth draoidheil na grèine
na rolladh gu luath dhan Earrach.

Solstice Wood

There is a spinney on the ridge
and I am certain
that it was always there.
When the winter solstice comes
and a red sphere falls behind trees,
I like to think
I am not entirely alone
but that other eyes, across time
are with me, and show the same pleasure
that this is the shortest day
as the druid wheel of the sun
rolls swiftly towards springtime.

Prestwick Airport

Here the world's great walked on our common ground,
though we had history before they came:
Wallace once stood upon a nearby mound
to watch the well-stocked barns of Ayr aflame.
When I was young they called it Orangefield:
Ball and McCudden used to fly from here,
flat western farmland of the fogless bield
long before radar made dark heaven clear.
Now to new fields the flying galleons sail,
tracing their glide-paths over city walls.
Where once the Sleeping Warrior marked the trail
the ghosts of queuing travellers haunt the halls.

But even here among the phantoms and the blues
Elvis touched Scotland once in GI shoes.

Colonel John*

I happened on Red John in the high country of France,
in immaculate braid as though he had never been
chased through the heather or starved by a moorland burn.
There was a glass before him and a bottle of wine to hand,
his hair a little greyer but seeming healthy enough.
We spoke of those sad and angry lines he made,
but the anger had gone and he smiles a calmer smile
The end will come by the sword or by simple time,
he said, *dispute is profitless, the years are victor.*
Soldiers and poets are fools like the rest of men;
princes may die in renown or in infamous beds.
But the end is the same and the end will come to all.
For what remains of man are his puny monuments.
Yet for all my days of blood I remain in the faith.

His eyes travelled over the water, beyond the sailing swans
to the teeth of the high rocks and the blue vault,
and he raised his glass to me, and sipped, and laughed.

* John Roy Stuart, Jacobite poet, soldier of France, died in exile 1752.

Dante

Nuair a bha Dante na sheasamh air an drochaid
saoil gur e Bèatris riomhach bha na bheachd?
Docha gu robh e smaoineachadh air Laideann
a thrèig e air son duain garga Flortentaich.

Is cò a sgriobhadh mar sin sa chainnt bheag shuarach
nach cluinnteadh riamh sa Roimh no Siracusa?
s nach tuigeadh fear dhiubh suas an Mediolanum?
Bha e cinnteach gun tigeadh fhuadach gu Ravenna.

Is a dh' ainneoin Bèatris is bàrdachd is gach uile ni
Guelphaich, Ghibellinaich, Clann Geal is Clann Dubh
chaochail e an Ravenna mu dheireadh thall
is leugh na sgriobh e Italia gu lèir.

Is thoisich iad air bruidhinn Florenteach,
gaol ac' air Ifrinn is Purgadair is Pàrras.
Tha a' chreatlach aige na laighe an Ravenna,
is muinntir Florentia glè farmadach m' a dheidhinn.

Dante

When Dante was standing on the bridge
do you think it was bonnie Beatrice he thought about?
More likely he was thinking about Latin
that he had deserted for rough Florentine.

And who would write like that in an odd little tongue
that wouldn't be heard in Rome or Syracuse
and that nobody in Mediolanum (Milan) would understand?
he was certain he would be exiled to Ravenna.

An in spite of Beatrice and poetry and everything else
Guelphs and Ghibellines, Clan White and Clan Black
he died in Ravenna at the latter end
and the whole of Italy read what he has written.

And they started to speak Florentine,
besotted with Hell and Purgatory and Paradise.
His skeleton lies there in Ravenna,
and the people of Florence are jealous about that.

Letter From Charlie Kelly

8th December 1854*

Dear Brother, I write you these few lines...

from these grim barracks where a grey Thames fog
clothes the December day broken by trumpets
calling us to parades, our only Advent.

Long looked for comes at last,
I am off tomorrow, bag and baggage...
on board the ship Indiana... there is no lies this time...

No lies this except from those who gain by war,
no lies but Queen and Empire, Queen and Country.

No lies this time for we have passed the Docter...
150 of us altogether, for the Crimea...

For all our poverty, big fellows with strong muscles
to dig the mines and saps, trenches, redoubts

... you need not write until you hear from me
after i land. I expected you would have wrote
before this time...

Forgive me what was to be forgiven;
bad debts, bad deeds, the taint of soldiery.

Give my respects to Mr Miller and Sam
and the rest fo the young men about the Townhead.

Who will not die in the bitter winter cold,
or of festering wounds on stinking palliases
far, far from the old Townhead and the warm hearth.

No more at present but remains yours aye,
Charles Kelly, R S & Miners, Brompton Barracks.

---

* The portions in italics are from a letter form Charles Kelly to his brother, my great-
great-grandfather.

Scotlit Cringe

(It has become unfashionable for Scots to speik, let alone write in native tongues)

It's even waur not dabblin in politicks,
yon's no for the likes o us – and as for poetrie
an siclike wark. Scots winna dae, ye see
a bard the day maun learn new-farrant tricks:
nae rime or ocht lik yon, nae beat that sticks
like bairnrimes dae in auld memorie.
Yon Scottish blauds will haurdlie airn a fee
gin ye're no yin a *London* critic picks.

Yon Langholm chiel, MacGrieve or whit-d'ye cry him
had ti get prentit first in fremit airts
New York it wes. Deavin fowk's lugs wi Scots!

Write Standard Panloaf English. Dinna try thaim
wi aa yon Burns-like an lug-fanklin lots.
Luik southarts gin ye'd be a bard-o-pairts

Creag Ealasaid

Bha Suibhne Geilt na shuidhe an seo
's a' gabail anail eadar Eireann 's Albainn
air mullach na carraige seo
no air iteal fad os cionn
guga is faoileag is farspag
eun dubh na sgadan, buthaid,
air là math as t-shamhradh
iarmailt glan os chionn,
Cluaidh feathach fo chois,
is e saor o chath, cìsean
toinisg, dalm-bheachd,
mithean is maithean
is luchd beulach politiceach.

Ailsa Craig

Crazy Sweeney sat here
taking his ease between Ireland and Scotland
on the summit of this rock,
or flying high above
gannet, gull and blackback
guillemot and puffin
on a fine summer's day,
clear sky above
Clyde calm below
and he free from battle, taxes,
common sense, bigotry,
semple and gentle,
and the pratings of politicians.

Mind Yir Taes

(Dangerous objects dumped carelessly off the Solway coast began to be washed ashore)

Jist aff the Mull thare's a muckle howe in the sea
Atween the Scottish the Irish shore
Some deep-doun girnel hes been caad ajee.
It skails oot shells that werna thare afore:
No clabbie-doos or buckies or siclike
That ye micht byle an fry an eat wi saut
Yon hairst that boaks up frae the Beaufort Dyke
Ye winna swage, een wi the best o maut
Dinna gae soomin doun bi Ballantrae
Or paiddlin near Portpaitrick – tell the wean –
Waur nor a scowder-stang thay'll gie ye pain.
Nae maitter tho – thay're ower faur awa
ti kittle taes doun in Westminster Haa.

Astar nam Faobh

Eadar Cul-'ian is Arainn
chan ann ach dusan mìle;
nuair a bha mi òg
bha Gàidhlig ac' an Seasgann s Cille Mhoire.

Air mùr Caisteal nan Cinneadaich
an diugh fhein sheas mi ag amharc,
thar uachdar feathach ciùin Chluaidh.
Chunnaic mi dusan mìle –
astar fada gu dearbh.

The Path of Spoils

Between Culzean and Arran
it's only a dozen miles;
when I was young
there was Gaelic in Shiskine and Kilmory:
from the battlements of the Kennedies' Castle
this very day I stood looking out
over the calm surface of Clyde.
I could see for a dozen miles,
a great distance indeed.

Arran

I sal gae back yae day
afore ma warld enns
ti Arran o the monie stags,
an the lang glens

For aye I mynd again
bluid-rid an gowden fire
o a simmer's deein suin
ayont Kintyre

Arran

I would go back some day
before my world ends
to Arran of the many stags
and the long glens.

For I recall again
scarlet and golden fire
in the summer's dying sun
beyond Kintyre.

Dinnae Say 'Aye' — Say 'Yes'*

Dinnae say 'aye' but say 'yes'
gin ye want ocht ye say ti be tentit
syne yir kinship will maitter the less
an ye'll no be sae bleck as ye're pentit

Carlo Porta an Guiseppe Belli
they didnae write proper Italian-
but the speik o the orra street fellie
the puir an the raplich rascallion.

But *Buffone* wad scrieve the fine stanza
in wards that he borried frae Dante,
nae *hidalgo* but mair Sancho Panza,
in stridlegs abuin Rosinante.

In oor ain bit Rab Burns and Rab Garie,
wad gar the strang Scots fit thegither,
but the pan-loaf, that Spondee will sair ye
gars London's best lugs gae a-swither.

Sae the twa Rabs, an Belli an Porta
whase flains aye steck hame whaur they're sent tae
sen the plebs ken sic wards are nae thorter
an will stound just as lang as thay're meant tae.

___

* a former injunction to Scots-speaking children at school

My Grannie had the Gaelic

My Grannie had the Gaelic,
but I don't have a word,
being brought up in the City
where such chat is thought absurd.
My dear old *faither* spoke Braid Scots
and not the Beebspeak tongue,
bit I soon learned to speak RP
to scale the topmost rung.

At Caledonian Happenings
I'm present to applaud
(with the City literati
I'm the nearest thing to God).
I claim to love our languages,
to hold the culture dear,
and turn up dressed in Highland style
to mark the passing year.

There's January Suppertime
among the Mice and Men:
A man's a Man for Aa That,
Tam o' Shanter and *Tam Glen*;
There's the *Stabbing of the Haggis*
and *The bashing of the Neaps*:
while its all right for an evening
I'm so glad its not for keeps.

But I write a little column
in the *Scottish Daily Moan*,
and tell my pawky little jokes:
Hoots mon! and *Pog mo thon*!
I knock these tongues for all I'm worth
it helps the paper sell,
to all the snobs in Scotland,
(and I'm paid for it as well.)

Lament for MacGreegor of Glenstrae:

Frae the Gaelic.

*(The chronicle o the Vicar o Fortingall: 1570. The vj da of
Apryill Gregor MacGregor of Glensra heddyt at Belloch anno
sexte an ten yeris.)*

Richt blithe upo yon Lammas morn
my luve and I did play,
but my puir hert wi dule wes worn
afore the bricht noonday.

Cursit the lairdlings and their freens
wha brocht me til this grief,
wha cam in traison tae my luve
and twined him lik a theif.

My een wad neer hae shed thir tears
nor wad thy sire be died,
gif there had been twal clansman here
wi Greegor at their heid.

His hause laid on an aiken clug,
his bluid skailt on the grun;
hid I a bicker of yon bluid
fain wad I drink it doun.

Wad my ain sire a leper wir,
Grey Colin seik wi plague
The Ruthven lassie wringan haunds
aside whaur they wir laid.

Grey Colin and Black Duncan baith
sae ticht I'd twine in airns
wi ilka Campbell in Taymooth
weel happit roon in chains.

Upo the green o Taymooth Tour
in wanrest I wad staund,
nae lock unruggit on my heid
nor skin upon my haund.

O gin I had the laverock's flicht
bauld Greegor's virr abune,
the tapmost stanes of Taymooth Tour
I'd caa doun til the grun.

Their wives are happit snug et hame
sleepan the nicht awa:
by my ain bed I bide my lane
until the daylicht daw.

Fain wad I be wi Greegor there
in muir and birk alane,
than beddit wi the Laird of Dall
in waas o aislar stane.

Fain hud I been wi Greegor
in an orra sark o hair,
than weiran silk and velvet
wi the laird of Dalach there.

Ba hu, ba hu, my son forfairn
sae weirdless and sae smaa
I fear ye'll time the tid, ma bairn,
o vengeance on thaim aa.

Singing

It was seldom calm; most night the usual wind
from Ireland across the machair, but no rain.
I walked in those light nights to the halfway inn
to drink myself singing. English words faded
as the long night wore on. A body could believe
the song would never die in spite of all.

Homeward in that late twilight; abbey walls
rose to the skyline on the further island.
Surely their songs were holier far than ours,
bawled out in drink in that rough hostelry?

But lonely there upon the morning shore,
knowing that in those taproom choruses
there was a yearning deep as sanctity.

King Lourie*

The King's hair is long
for his barber is slain,
he calls me to comb out
and sleek his great mane.

Tall Tree of the Harpstrings
now answer me fair,
why does he slay barbers
who trim his long hair?

*His crown is of gold
and his scepter of pearls,
but the ears of a donkey
are hid by his curls.*

What then shall I do
when I barber his head?

*Make sure you are shriven
for soon you'll be dead.*

*   from Keating's Gaelic tale of Labhraidh Loingseach.

Solas

to the late Sorley Maclean

Thum mi òrdag sa chuan
far an do sheòl mo dhaoine
nuair a bha birlinn aca.
mus na chaill iad ràmh is siùil
nuair a chaochail Alasdair is Bhaltair.*
Bhithinn a' sealltainn thar fairrge
air taobh thall Arainn gu Chinntìre
na mheur fada a' comharrachadh
oirthir Eireann air fàire.

Bha mi 'feuchainn bhòids ùr
bho Linne Ratharsaidh mu thuath,
a nochd dhomh combaist is acainn,
is a sheall dhomh ciamar a sheòlainn
gun eagal air camas nan stuadh
air ais gu Alba a b'fheàrr leam.

Solas

I dipped a finger in the sea
where my people had sailed
when they had a galley,
before they lost oar and sails,
with the death of Alasdair and Walter.*
I would look across the sea
on the far side of Arran to Kintyre
a long finger pointing
to Ireland's coast on the horizon;

I was trying a new voyage
but I had no seamanship
or chart to keep me on the proper course.

Then I found a new beam of sunlight
from the sea of Raasay to the North
that revealed to me compass and rigging,
and showed me how I could sail
without fear on the gulf of the sea
back to the Scotland I preferred.

---

*   Alexander Montgomerie and Walter Kennedy, poets who knew the Gaelic of the
Carrick district of Ayrshire.

In Memoriam Duncan Ban MacIntyre

(Born Glenorchy 1724 died Edinburgh 1812)

When they took away his hills
Fair Duncan of the Songs
became Grey Duncan of the doggerel.

When he high passes were closed to him
the Misty Corrie and Glenorchy
of the green grassy knowes,
they gave him a tricorn, a halberd
and hodden grey breeches for the Sabbath day.

The prototype of Heiland Polisman,
he sat off-duty in their dingy howffs,
in Canongate ingle-neuks
fisting a brandy-glass for city sprigs to fill
delighted to send a Gaelic poet up
to shout his metres from remembered bens.

'Why yes, your honour, I'll make a verse for you
sa Ghàidhlig a dhuine is taigh na galla ort *
and here's your very good health, sir.'

*'Is truagh nach robh mi air Buachaill Eite
is an sneachd gu ruig mo shleisdean
is a h-uile Gall a tha an Duneidinn
as mo dhèidh is iad casruisgte.'* **

Fair Duncan of the Songs
Grey Duncan of the doggerel,
the fate of all bards
when time takes the hill from them.

---

*   In Gaelic sir, and a plague take you.

** tis sad that I'm not on Buachaill Etive/and the snow up to my thighs,/and every
       lowlander in Edinburgh/at my back and they barefooted.

     The tale goes that this reply was made to certain clever young gentlemen who could
     not understand Gaelic.

Covenanter

They shot Will Graham before his mother's house;
doctrinal dispute: Home Calvin, Away Cranmer.
Damning and blinding dragoons ignorant of Rome or Geneva
tested his orthodoxy with prayer book and bullet.

Here among summer grass the interest blooms again;
tourists bend double to read the faded glyphs:
for kirk and covenant; now knowing little of either,
they pause beside Crossmichael's quaint round steeple.

On the dark moss-hags saints and dragoons sleep sound
rooled tight together, blent to a common leaven,
a spark in the heads of those who consider causes,
worry on crucifix, bonnet, knee, confession.

The rest don't care about it. The curious kirk
attracts the eye, leaving the soul unlit.
Bullet and test live on in the mind of God;
the covenanter's cause sleeps as sound as Will.

Threave Castle

The earls are gone from this abolished tower
islanded gauntly in the stream's embrace;
a breached and roofless watershed of power,
broken bleak walls of an old broken race.
One to courageous dying turned his face,
charged an unconquerable paynim band
throwing his King's heart towards the holy land.

A lesser stayed at home, his soul immured
in this most grim and cruel unyielding stone,
daily his murderous tyranny ensured
the corpse that dangled by the tower door.
Another chased a hundred mile or more
a king's enquirer from the castle gate:
the brigand sovereign of wild estate.

Then at the last, their blood dismantled them,
smashed the dark wall beside the timeless stream.
Old pride grown stale tumbled them down again,
a cankered enclave of a larger scheme.
Who stand at evening on this bank and dream
false tales of chivalry in gleaming plate,
weigh them against the corpse above the gate.

The Ballant of Condullie Rankine

Condullie Rankine gaed ti war
at the battle o Shirramuir, man,
ti fecht thare for MacLean an Mar
wi claymore straucht and sure, man.
Condullie wes a piper bauld
skeilie on drone an chanter,
but aye in Mull the tale is tauld
aboot his sair mishanter.

Like ilka piper o his day
a weill-kent *duine-uasal*,
he played (but no the Sabbath day)
ceòl mòr in Duart Castle;
't wes needfu when he gied a tune
ti oxter thaim an play thaim
but wi him cam a reid-haired loun
whase task wes ti convey thaim.

Condullie piped the Clan MacLean
atour the hills an heather
an played *Auld Stewart's Back Again*
for twintie miles thegither;
aye swankin at his heels in glee
the fernie-tickilt callant
whase conduck on that day maun be
the subjeck o this ballant.

Thay cam doun ti the lawlan plain
wi *caismeachd* soundin shrilly
Condullie aised the bagpipe's wame
an gied thaim ti his gillie:
syne gowpit doun a braith or twa
drew forth his blade for battle
an lowpt wi Clann *illeathan gu brath!*
intil the muskets' brattle.

Neist cam a muckle cannon-rair
Auld Clootie's lugs wad deave, sir,
but reid-heid dinna bide lang thare
afore he thocht ti leave, Sir,
he didnae leave the bagpipes thair
(the better for oor story)
but bare thaim frae yon sad affair
full dreel ti Tobermorie.

Condullie birled his michtie blade
dealt oot his dunts richt sairlie
til aa at yince his chieftan bade
him soond retreat oot fairlie.
Condullie gaed ti pipe the tune
ti whaur he'd left weill-gairdit
his staund o pipes an fand the loun
wi instrument, depairtit.

Condullie sware baith loud and lang
yon *balach* he wad flype, sir;
the road ti Mull wes dreich an lang
wantin the mirrie pipes, sir.
Doun thair lang nebs the tacksmen glared,
the laird fufft in his tartans,
Condullie, silent, hameward fared
wi lugs as reid as partans.

A wickit bard thare wes in Coll
eke o the Clan MacLean, sir,
wha socht ti tuim his stowp o gall
on puir Condullie's name, sir,
He hated chanter, drone and bag
detestit thae that played thaim
an whan he heard the pipers brag
wi shairp satire he flayed thaim.

'What think ye o the pipes, *a ghraidh*,
o yon Condulllie Rankine?'
In battle whan he laid thaim bye,
straucht hamewards thay cam spankin
raxed oot thair drones lik airms an legs
an swithlie fled disaster,
lowpt on a lubber lounie's back
ti hoy thaim hame the faster.

Nou pipers, gin ye'd pipe a tune
at ceilidh or in battle,
ne'er truist a thowless, plookie loun
ti mind yir pipes an chattels;
gin ye gae aff ti tak yir dram –
in this ye maunna swither
tak baith the pipes an loun alang
an hae yir dram thegither.

The Woodland of Cross

(from the Gaelic of Hector MacLeod fl. 1750)

My pleasure, my joy, my delight
and my being's care
should the clergy such pleasure indict
I'd still bide there.

Sweet tune of harp and lyre,
droned pipe well played,
yet sweeter the birds in choir,
in this woodland shade.

Sure stronghold of trees,
from the world's bane;
right thought and the heart at ease
in yon woodland fane.

Branches of fruit and flowers,
each taste and scent,
make peaceful the hours
in the wood's conent.

Music of the world's play
when the city calls
is banished forever away
by the sounding falls.

Firm your foot on rock –
how sure its tread,
untired in its walk,
thro the river glade.

White front, silver scale
the flecked fishes leap
nor do myriads fail
their bright tryst to keep.

Unibike at the Festival

Aa thir graund ploys and players in the toon –
Jist bi the Mound a chiel on a unibike
Echt feet abuin the grunn, a Cockney tyke,
Gies us the patter, birlin roon an roon
Ye'd think him jist aboot ti cletter doon:
No him. Jooglin an aipple an twa shairp dirks
As braisant as the Deil an aa his Warks
An aabodie cheerin the cantrips o this loun

Keepin the dirkies gaun, an haein a bite
Oot o the aipple an nivver lossin his grip
or faain doon aff yon unibike affair.

Gin I could maister yon I'd drive thaim gyte –
Wi sangs an sonnets I fairlie wad let rip
Et poetrie readins, echt feet abuin the flair.

A Song to the Highland Dress

(From the Gaelic of John MacCodrum, 1693?-1779. After the Disarming Act of 1748 which forbade its use.)

Sick and sore am I, worn and weary
walking no more since my limbs are bound.
Cursed be the king who stretched our stockings
down in the dust may his face be found.
The length of our legs in these lubber wrinkles
scarce does such gear beome a man:
better we loved our graceful short-hose
from heel to garter but a span.

Coats he'll allow us with tails a-flapping
shoes he'll leave us by the score,
but treat us with no trace of honour,
grabbing our gear to make us poor;
worse than all this he forces backsides
into these niggard peasant breeches,
knowing the spreading of the comely tartan
meant more to us than our riches.

In this clumsy cassock I'm tangled nightly
can't stretch my legs, no wink of sleeping.
Better the ease of ten yards single
that in the morning I'd be pleating –
a lightsome dress, kept wind and rain off
every gallant lad who had it:
the curse of the two worlds upon
the mean usurper who forbade it.

No summer dress that can beat the tartan,
lighsome and cheerful when its snowing
the favoured garb of hardy warrior
pain for its lack impedes their going;
the sheltering cloth of splendid Gaels,
Lord! it's a blow that pains us quite
that they should ban the belted plaid
to kill our fashion out of spite.

You would seldom see a mother's son
that strolled the street or on parade
more handsomely in his native dress
than those of Gaeldom's sons arrayed,
with tartan gathered at waist and pleated,
broadsword and musket behind shield,
pistols that never would misfire
what foeman would face him on the field?

How trimly the blue bonner sits
on locks that tumble from his head,
short coat and kilt around bare thighs
marching to meet the foeman's blade
in bloody furious battle-mood,
to crush those uniformed in red
strong men that swing their lusty blade
to leave each neck without a head.

When the Gael gathers on the field
with gleaming helmet, Spanish blade
how dearly then their blood will flow
and all Culloden's debts be paid,
no man of honour, plundered there
or led away in captive chains,
but he shall learn how well redeemed
by alien gore are all his pains.

When Scottish men shall hear your tread
they'll swiftly join the figured banner
Clan Donald marching as is their wont,
to trim red-coats in the tailor's manner,
not sewing up but cutting cloth,
with blades whose aim is sure and certain
to claim a debt of ears and skulls,
for every check within the tartan.

What grief our dress has changed its shaping,
well may our vengeance fall on London,
fighting like lions in that place
so Geordie shall his throne abandon,
go off to find his native dwelling,
and his young prince be swiftly fettered.
When Charlie's safely throned as monarch
the tartan's value will be bettered.

Life is a prison when plaids are lacking
we'll send a prayer up to restore 'em.
When half a million Frenchmen come,
with general Charlie there before them
the Sutherland tweed they'll soon be waulking
engage in battle wise and sudden,
when the sows' singed and boiled her litter,
broadsword and tartan no more forbidden.

When I was Young

Easment of sadness in early rising,
on a May morning and I in Os,
one to another the cattle calling,
the dawn arising above the Storr;
a spear of sunlight upon the mountains
saw the last shadow of darkness gone,
the blithsome lark high above me singing
brought back to mind days when I was young.

A memory mingled with joy and sadness,
I lack the words that can tell them true,
each case and change of my mind and body,
far from the glen whose bright peace I knew;
the river rippling so gently seawards,
my own speech echoed in the streamlet's flow
sweet sang the mavis in budding branches,
to wake the memories of long ago.

In careless joy I would roam the moorland,
the heather tips brushing on my dress,
through mossy knowes without help of footgear,
when ice was forming on the lochan's face;
seeking the sheep on the mountain ridges,
light as the snipe over meadow grass,
each mound and lochan and rolling hollow...
these are the memories to time that's past.

I bring to mind all the things I did there
that will not fade till my story's end,
walking in winter to prayer or wedding,
my only lantern a peat in hand;
the splendid youngsters, with song and dancing...
gone are their days now and sad the glen;
now Andrew's croft under shrouding nettles
brings back to mind how our days were then.

How I would travel each glen and hill-top,
herding the cattle with tranquil mind,
with lively youngsters now long in exile,
a sturdy breed without foolish pride.
Pasture and ploughland now heath and rushes,
where sickle swept and the sheaf was tied;
could I see dwellings again and people
as once in youth there I'd gladly bide.

There I would climb on the mountain shoulder,
to take my ease on the grassy height;
my thought would leap in a blaze of wonder,
such beauty lying below my sight:
the royal thistle and the yellow primrose,
the golden blossom of sweet Saint Bride,
each joyous leaf under dew at evening
brings back a memory of youth's delight.

I turned my back on that fragrant homeland,
to take the vessel that needs no breeze,
but sounds a horn to put in motion
and set her course from the island seas;
My heart was crushed and the tears were flowing
going to a place lacking song or peace,
where there's no thistle or nodding gowan,
rush bank or heather or grassy lease.

The Poet in Canada

(From the Gaelic of John MacLean, 1787-1848)

I'm all alone in this gloomy woodland,
my mind is troubled, I sing no song:
against all nature I took this place here
and native wit from my mind has gone.
I have no spirit to polish poems,
my will to start them is dulled by care;
I lose the Gaelic that was my custom
in yon far country over there.

I cannot muster my thoughts I order
though making songs was my great delight;
there's little joy comes to smoor my sadness
with no companion to ease my plight;
each night and day, in each task I turn
to the ache of memory grows more nnd more;
I left my dear land beside the ocean
and now no sea laps my dwelling's shore.

It is no wonder I should be grieving
behind these hills in a desert bare,
in this hard country of Barney's River
a few potatoes my only fare;
I must keep digging to win bare living
to hold these wild threatening woods at bay;
my strength alone serves till sons reach manhood
and I may fail long before that day.

This is a country that's hard and cruel,
they do not know it who journey still;
evil the yarns of the smooth-tongued coaxers
who brought us hither against our will;
yet if they profit it won't advance them,
may they not prosper despite their loot,
the cursed wretches who drive out people
since first this Clearance was set afoot.

Strong is the promise that they will make you
this place's virtues they'll loudly boast;
your friends, they'll say, now grow rich and prosper
not lack for those things that men want most.
They'll fill your ears with each lying rumour
to make you follow them where they will;
where they appear, few escape them safely,
fortunate they who evade them still.

Drovers of men who come to seek you
will seal their bargain with a lie,
no single word of truth they're telling
for what their tongues say, their hearts deny;
loud is their boasting of what this land holds
each thing that's rarest, waits to be won,
but when you come here, little you'll see then
but great tall forests that steal the sun.

When comes the winter, a bitter season
the forest branches are clothed in snow,
and no plain cloth is defence against it,
thigh deep and thick on the ground below;
but clouted moccasins and double stockings
and leather thongs are our forest boots;
rawhide and fur are our latest fashions
ripped from the backs of the forest brutes.

Without true learning and skill in dressing
I would be frozen from brow to chin,
the stinging winds of the freezing northland
kill feet and hands did I let them in;
a frightful cold takes the edge from axes,
the bite of frost blunts the hardest blade;
no smith or forge here to heal spoiled metal
so fire must melt ere one notch be made.

The month of May and the first of summer,
my strength is drained by the blazing sun,
that wakes from the winter the forest creatures
where they lay weakly in den and run;
the prowling bears rise from winter slumbers,
a roaming band that's a sore mischance;
the snouted fly with his store of poison
deals wounds unceasing from his sharpened lance.

He stabs my face with an eager malice
till with his venom my eyelids swell;
there's no escaping his burning juices
that gall my eye like a flame of hell;
I have not space to relate the boldness
of each fowl crawler that seeks its prey;
like to the plagues that the Pharoh suffered,
my mean condition from day to day.

In this wide world there come many changes;
I little knew in that other land,
how fond my dreams at the time of leaving
that in due time I'd be rich and grand;
a turn I took that was not for profit,
a lying hope made me cross the sea.
This land of trees is no land of freedom,
no herd gives milk nor flock their wool for me.

There's many a shift I must turn my hand to
before I'm sure of my daily fare;
rough is the task till I win its profit
and make arrangement for needful gear:
stacking the tree-trunks to set them burning
lights fire in sinews across my back,
and like a man who's been sweeping chimneys,
my body changes to sooty black.

Great were the tales that they told in Scotland
their falsehood proved by our sorry lot;
I've never handled a silver dollar
although I'm told that they can be got.
A deal is made, but there's no coin passes,
though you have bargained that cash be paid,
they'll take your gear but they'll pay no money,
for flour and butter is all their trade.

I see no market, I see no fair day,
no wealthy drovers of cattle here,
nought in our townland but want and shortage
that can't be bettered for lack of gear.
No cause of envy, our sorry debtors
whose trifling treasures don't match the score,
head hung in shame and a debtor's prison
when they have rouped all the meagre store.

Before the case ever reaches courtroom
be sure the roup will increase the debt;
the law they get from the jury's handling
makes sure the reiving's not over yet;
through our poor country the sheriff travels,
by the court's warrant he hounds the poor;
I live in fear that I'll see him bringing
his debtor's summons towards my door.

I cannot say in these simple verses,
no skill have I in such words as tell
to distant friends all the thoughts that fill me
of yon dear land where I used to dwell.
But let who read this heed well its meaning
and give no ear to the liars there
who boast this land only but to hook you
and trim their profits from your passage fare.

Though I've been diligent in the writing
its taken me a full month or more
to set to rights all the things I'm thinking,
to shape in words all that grieves me sore;
in my soul's depth such a sadness fills me,
each weary day adds its hours of strife,
no joyful song fills this forest prison
that hold me fast for what's left of life.

How changed my custom from my youth's gladness,
the sounding days round each merry board;
joyful my heart in each happy meeting
our days a-flying while our spirits soared;
now since I left you my heart beats sadly:
the hot salt tears on my cheeks were shed,
on Thursday last as I saw the packet,
her head turned eastward and her canvas spread.

Clerk ti the Marquis

(Owerset frae the Milanese o Carlo Porta, 1775-1822)

Ay-Ay-Sir, maister, are ye no a Marquis
Mark-us-a-doun, mark-me-youse-yins?
An I'm jist common Chairlie for ma sins
that hes nae fancy duddies ti remark-us.

An ye growe smuith an creeshie in yir carcase
an aye growe fatter wi yir baws for brains
while I maun tyauve ti keep fleish on ma banes
an hae ti shift ma airse ti whaur the wark is.

An you athoot the harns ti read an write
or speik ti lick-ma-dowps that beck an bou –
deaved wi the fletherin tales ye hear thaim tell.

An whit a weird is mine, gey near gaen gyte
bent ower yir documents the lang day thro
athoot 'guid-day' frae a gomeril like yirsel.

Canto Macaronach

A Caledonian Canto

Write down with learning and loving knowing
the story of their people, their high song
and never in Great Colin's ear be sowing [1]
a twisted verse whose metre limps along.

Sgrìobh go fiosach fireòlach
a seanchas is a gcaithrèim;
nà beir duan air mhìsheòladh
go a lèigheadh go Mac Cailèin. [2]

Is e tha ceàrr le siorrachd Albainn
gu h-àraidh measg fhilidh ar linn fhèin
cèisdean mar 'Co a nis leughas mo dhàn?'
no 'De an cainnt is cò a thuigeas i?'
Is saor o feadhainn gann is onorach,
ni tair gun stad air cainnt an sinnsre. [3]

An ocht in Scots the day jist willna dae
athoot some column-scrievin cockapentie
makkin wee baurs for scruntie hamebred snobs
wha haena heard o Wattie, Will or Rab. [4]

*   *   *   *   *   *   *   *   *   *   *   *

They'll crash your door when evenings fall
to eat you out of house and hall,
said Finlay of Glen Dochart.

A ranting, roving idle crew
who'll pay you but a song or two,
said Finlay of Glen Dochart.

I'll not attempt their pedigree
nor tell their doubtful history,
said Finlay of Glen Dochart.

With dogs at heel, a hungry horde
who plunder folk of bed and board,
said Finlay of Glen Dochart.

But mind, for all their ruffian state,
the songs they sing are worth their meat,
said Finlay of Glen Dochart.

So see you write down all their rhymes
and mine as well, for sadder times,
said Finlay of Glen Dochart.

Finlay still lives in a few Scottish minds
but certainly not many, though the *duanaire*
still sits on shelves and gathers Scottish dust,
which barring Burns would seem to be the fate
of Caledonian poets generally.

MacDiarmid knew of him and Deòrsa Mòr could quote him [5]
Deibhidhe, Ae freislighe, Rannaigheacht Mhòr [6]
are dead and gone from all but scholarship;
hardly surprising in an age that hates
all but its own facile, dry cleverness,
affects disdain of Petrarch for its own dull lines
sprawling sans song or vision across pages.

Tha iomadach sgonna-bhàrd mabach amaideach
na shuidhe san àrd-cathair a ni geolam
a' bruidhinn mu 'bhoidhchead ar bàrdachd Gàidhlig'
is chan fhoghlum iad aon fhacal singilte dhith.
Maithean a mheasas an taobh a muigh a mhàin:
Clan Sud is *Clan Seo* is Clan Sìos leis a' Ghàidhlig,
breacan MacBuggins is Nogginson mun tòn. [7]

Thank God for Marsali Kennedie Fraser
who saved for us each grand old song
who cut grace notes with gelding razor:
yon *port-a-bheulairs* got it wrong. [8]

Away from pentatonic whining
of draughty *bothan* in the west
in city drawing room reclining
the songs (in RP) ring out the best.

Horì horo mo chailean donn
cha teid mi idir thall mu thuath,
an Eilean I cha tog mi fonn
is cha tog piob mo chridhe gu luath. [9]

Whit is't that gars ye sit an scrieve
sic crabbit lines in yon auld wey?
sae fowk sal ken at it's still vieve
on tungs frae Solway tae the Spey.

Agus is iomadh duan fhathast
a cluinnear thall san eilean siar,
is bardachd ùr a' tighinn an dràsd
bho fheadhainn òg is daoine liath. [10]

That's not the problem, verses still are made
In 'older tongues' the more indiginous
(Lost are the words the Beaker Men displayed
The *Gwr y Gogledd* nobles gone from us) [11]
But audiences in city halls arrayed
Think native tongues are hardly worth a cuss.
Northern demotic English hardly passes
Without a sniffing from their upper classes.

* * * * * * * * * * *

The certain aim of each language
under the sun is to communicate
our growing vision to one another.
To lay bare our thoughts
and the inclination of our hearts
towards deed and conduct;
swiftly to amend our defects,
and with 'the calves of our lips'
to praise God of the Elements
it is the great high purpose
so to give praise.

Man is the single living creature of reason
the divine will gave him
the gift of speech of his mouth,
that marked him out from every other animal;
o great splendid prize
the shaping of his own image.
Had he been born dumb
and his tongue dead in his mouth
that would have been the bitter dregs of grief.
Better by far never to have been.

* * * * * * * * * *

There's many a tongue
from Babel's tower
but over all
victorious Gaelic...

And still alive
its fame undimmed
in spite of slander
and alien ignorance.

Scotland spoke it
even Lowland bodies,
our nobles, princes
and peerless dukes.

In the king's council
at the court's conclusion
it was polished Gaelic
unravelled the knot. [12]

* * * * * * * * * * *

An then, guidsakes, mynd on that ither crew
at ken nae tung but Boarding Schuil Vernacular
wha seem tae thenk that Chaxpur spak RP [13]
an think a ferlie when some nordern chiel
maks Dame MacBeth yaise Scottish vocables
An no the phonemes Guid Queen Vic *received.*
But thare's an een mair tapsalteerie notion
brocht on bi literarie *men o pairts*
soukin up ti whit's thocht The Guid and Great,
cheepin awa in peelie-wallie mymins
o suddron Hame-Coontie-Eton-an-Oxbridge-speik
that willna come oot richt for aa thair fash.
Weill nou: what sai thai? Thai sai! lat thaim sai –
gin thay'll no ettle ti gar ither bodies,
or duddie weans ti speik their crackjaw patter.

* * * * * * * * * * * * * *

Against big mouths the little tongues must wage
a constant war on ignorance in high places;
it does not take a wise man long to gauge
brains that are frozen hard behind the faces
of those whose fashion always is to rage
against the common herd whose tongues show traces
of never having graced a Private School
where RP phonemes serve to hide the fool.

Quango and clique where power and money lies
and where Sir-Humphrey-Speak is cultivated,
are seldom gaffered by the good and wise
for in such gangs you'll find the dedicated
moring-coat monoglot who always tries
to halt the course that's ever indicated
from *Beowulf* to Beebspeak and arrange
that what's 'correct' today will never change.

But where two tongues develop side by side
the more intelligent know more than one,
what though the *ruling* argot stretches wide
the language of the heart is much more fun:
therein the greater wisdom may abide
though only those who speak them both can know
what subtleties the lexis holds below.

When once at *Troye the borg brittened and brent*
This was a far cry from Old Vic's RP
or her cruel fader dide her for to hente
as far again from what is thought to be
the modern 'proper speech'. Tongues are soon bent
to other fashions in a year or three,
case-endings perish, the subjunctives flee
while *less* and *fewer* lose their subtlety.

Why in The Scottish Play the bloody dame
Old Mac and Banquo, Fleance and the rest
should speak RP with vowels that see quite lame:
why audiences in knightly tones addressed
should shun more northern variants of the same
has always seemed to me, calmly assessed
a piece of London Town One-Upmanship
that would have given the Warwick bard the pip.

Guidsakes, yae luk at the Establissment
sud pit the hames on yon cockapentie thocht.

* * * * * * * * * * * *

How many of the language purists know
that *pylgeint* comes from *pulicantio*
Roman reveille, soldiers' sparrow-fart,
Old Taffy's *dagreu* are Homer's *dakrua*:
Tears, idle tears, and some know what they mean –
I dash my staff in wrath upon the ground
at August Twelfth birdshots in philabegs
who do not know *Buachaill* is *Boukolos*. [14]
Dull criticasters limiting all speech
who cage up poetry in castrated lines
mo mhile mallachd on their gelded codes. [15]

Not every Roman spoke as Virgil wrote
Not all Italians ape the Florentine.
Silone speaks for all who crave their own:

The Fontamaresi do not speak Italian
Italian is just words we learn at school
as one learns Esperanto, French and Latin.
Italian's a strange lingo learned by rule,
the tricks of grammar, dictionary-pages
that have no code of reference to us;
not being the tongue of peasant loves or rages.
But when at last we take the exile's bus
to busy Rome, at last we realize
it comes to us with collars, shoes and ties. [16]

Mo al parol agli aslonga e' temp...
Ma le parole dilatanto il tempo...
As Bellosi says: the words expand the time.

* * * * * * * * * * * *

I ha mi Freud an allem gha, mi Herz
an alle duften, aller Schoni g'labt.

I hae ma joy in aathing, an ma hairt
in ilka scent an ilka beautie hapt.

Is gasda leam gach rud, agus mo chrìdhe
air ùrachadh le cùbhras agus maiseachd. [17]

None deny Homer for a mix of tongues
Herodotus for *barbarous dialect,*
Or place a ban on those Bucolic Songs:
No prudes or *elocutionists* object
To rustic rudeness or to Dorian twangs
Until our starveling native bards project
In homebred *langues* to illustrate despair.
Then pedant noses tilt for *purer* air.

Ochon a rì, chan fhaigh mi tàmh
a' feuchainn na mo dhuan fhin –
a chur tri chainnt air an aon ràmh
rud nach fasanta nar linn... [18]

Here in old Caledonia, wild and stern
no laurels, bay or myrtle wreath you'll earn
by crambo-clinking in Old Standard Habbie
or singing native strains (apart from Rabbie).

Twa hunner deid Scots poets spin lik peeries
whan Januar wins blaw in thir windie speeches
(God, ye can buy thaim prentit in a series!)
while ZZyne for syne rings oot in fremit reaches.

Agus ar cainnt as sine, Gàidhlig bhochd
le craiceann fhiacal chaidh i às an diugh,
a dh'ainneoin iomadh mi-rùn agus lochd.
Gu ma fada beò i, canain ar cheud-chliù. [19]

Nou Wattie Kinnidie *de Schliochd MacUalraig*
I conjure the, thow hungert heland gaist. [20]

Speik ower the lang years tae this modern breed
that carries nocht but Inglis in its heid.

Thou lufis nan Irishce, elf, I understand [21]
Bot it suld be all trew Scottis mennis lede;
It was the gud language of this land,
And Scota it causit to multiply and sprede...

Thow tynt cultur, I have cultur an pleuch...

It all depends on when your folks came over
if with King Fergus then you'll be alright – [22]
the Pict admixture makes you Scottish quite,
but from the Tattie Blight you can't recover.

Even if your lot are somewhere in the middle
between King Fergie and the British Raj
you can't dodge flute and shamrock, sash and badge,
or play mere Scottish reels upon your fiddle...

Celtic's a word that strangely raises
weird images within the Scottish psyche.
In Mungo's dear green place of displaced peasants
from the kingdom of Coel Hen,
from Kennedy's Carrick and Suibhne's Galloway
from reek-filled blackhouses emptied by factors
of alien Dukes for sheep and deer-forests,
antipathy to Celts is passing strange,
when Ringan-Ninian fosters jarring sects. [23]

But not all that strange when a Scottish child
may know how bloody minded Bluff King Hal
topped and tupped many a wife and bluffed the Pope,
but walks through Elderslie and knows not Wallace.
an English axe makes Mary queen of Scots:
Six minus five makes Jamie *England's* king.

* * * * * * * * * * * *

Good Blantyre Doctor Livingstone we presume
was holier that MacDhunleibhe, Islay bard. [24]
When you ask for the poetry of William Livingstone
Make sure you do it in an undertone.
The Islay tailor in his Glasgow slum
wrote lines too Caledonian for some
the flame of wrath in his *Fios chun a' Bhaird* [25]
to all but Gaeldom burns a little hard.

(It's not that William was exactly *banned*
but hated London rule, you understand:
couldn't thole *North Britons* claiming Scottish roots –
he thought of them as licking English boots.)

Though the sunlight rays are spreading
heaven's comfort on the land,
Now the shieling's herd is lowing
full in fold the yearlings stand:
people now are scarce in Islay,
there the sheep find life less hard
all around I hear and see them –
bear my message to the bard.

Am I a fool to be concerned with words?
There have been fools for love and power and gold
My foolishness is not the worst of these.

What is it makes a Scot?
No geography alone
nor the mere proclamation
divorced from loyalty to Scottish things:
not once a year Burnolatry
devoid of an understanding
to what Burns thought and wrote.
Not ignorance of Scottish poetry

beyond the maunderings of MacGonagle,
tartan-arsed *Roamings in the Gloaming*
and total ignorance of all the rest.

Ma's Goill, a ghaoil, ma's Gaidheil sinn
dh'àraich ise sinn. [26]

Weill ye kent the leid of Wull Dinbaur
the freedom sang o Barbour.
Hou monie Scottish bairns still ken it?
Ah freedom is a nobyll thing
freedom mayss man to haiff lyking

Cha b'àrd do cholann,
ach chunnaic mi athach nad spioraid,
air sràidean Duneidinn
is Cinntire uaine nad inntinn. [27]

The Craig an the Heids o Ayr,
the bights o Donegal
kyle o Kilbrennan an the comb o Arran
the race o watters on the sea o Moyle:
aye in yir een in Dunedin's dowie howffs.

Though their minds are on lesser things
You are not forgotten, nor the noble words
poured out for Scottish ears in their three tongues.

Agus ma bhios an cluasan air an lìonadh
le neo-shuim is briagan coimheach
cha b'thusa is coireach, A Dheòrsa.
Gach bliadhna a nis bidh feadhainn
a' cruinneachadh air a' mhòintich
mu thimchioll Carragh Uisdein:
is e àiridh air mòr-shluagh.
Ach chaneil carragh air a thogail
dhuit fhein a Dheòrsa ach d'obair fhèin.
Foghnaidh sin, gu dearbh. [28]

And the tung o Jamie Saxt aye crines
ablo a snirtin bing o cockapenties.

But yet the mind of Homer is not smothered
Nor is Dunbar drowned under the weight of dunces.

O alas for you, Scotland
for the goal of your thinking,
for the proof of your choosing
that has brought all destruction!
For a Government's greed
for each one who supports it –
they have fished for your greed
to foster your quarrels. [29]

Is e ceusadh an spioraid
as cràiteach san là seo
g'eil ar dùthaich air mùchadh
fo seasgachd is baoghaltach
gach baraile gun sgrùdadh;
chan fhiach dhaibh foghlam,
tha foighidinn a dhìth orr'
s iad a' caomhnadh an cainnt
o'n s cho gann leò an stòr dhith.

Gun Ghàidhlig no Scot-bheurl'
s iad a' gleac le cainnt-Lunainn,
chur an seacaidean Sass'nach;
beachd-smuaintean na h-Alba
Is fheàrr leò rosg geàrrt'
an toimhseachan gun fhuasgladh
is mur dean sinn mar sin
theid ar chur chur chun an t-siteig. [30]

An gin ye ettle ocht in guid Scots
still wi's thare's aye the *dull conceited hashes*
tae tell ye aa that but for Januar Suppers
the tung o the *Machair Gallda* is stane died,
whan aa aboot yir lugs are deaved wi't
in onie howff frae Drummore tae Peterheid.

Adapt! adapt! fashion's for Mawket Fawces
point your nose southwards, where the boys done well,
rhyme *law* with *poor* and tell your *Seketary*
to sloane it *proply* so that those Paw Cheps
in Indiar, Africar, Australiar and Americar
know where the loom of language spins its thread,
thin-drawn, avoiding archaisms and borrowings,
demotic speech, inversion, foreign tropes,
allowing hacks in the navel-scanning metropolis,
Doctor Glaurhowkers of Puddockhole University,
snooty elocutionists aping lordly noises,
back-bench pontificators, fashionable yowlers,
criticasting clowns in 'quality' journals,
to put your head in branks and clamp your tongue,
teach you contempt for hearty honest speech,
the parallel tongue, the colourful variant.

If you can keep your lisp when all about you
are losing theirs, you'll be a pseud, my son.

In 'Scottish' poetry now it's strongly hinted
this is the mode to take if you'd be printed,
based on what's most approved in Southern taste –
where strongly Jockish manners are a waste
of time for any bard who sets his cap
at selling hard-backs south of Watford gap:
make sure your 'verse' has neither sense nor form,
avoid emotion, dodge all stress and storm,
read up what's what, devise your 'market plan':

if you'd be published, never ryhme or scan –
avoid iambus, dactyl and spondee
for modern works must seem completely free
of metre, meaning, meat and common sense
(for more *uncommon* kind is no defence).
Never read Hardy, Byron, Dryden, Pope –
to ape such metrics would confine your scope;
avoid inverted lines, used much of old;
don't, like Will Shakespeare, use re-minted gold
for smooth as monumental alabaster's
no simile for a modern criticaster.
Never go in for polyglot abandon
use only lexis listed pure in London,
avoiding words thought much too Caledonian,
contrived Byronic desperate rhymes like 'phoney 'un'
to fill a hole – although the phrase might fit you
half-read anthologisers will omit you,
and never, never in poetic writing
go in for satire, irony, or flyting –
for that old adage 'if the cap fits, wear it',
wont do you any good – too many share it.
Last but not least, if you can find the fee,
Creative writing is a 'must' degree.
Twelve terms of listening to the tutor's patter
makes you a bard. Mere talent doesn't matter.

Agus an uair a chì thu
croitear bochd ag obair
le Gàidhlig air a theanga,
dean cinnteach 's bi ri fealla-dhà
is tu gun fhacal dearg dhith,
an sin bi duais gàire leat,
bho umaidhean na droch-Bheurla. [31]

Whan ye hear auld lyart bodies o the toun
gien thair crack et the baur o a Cougate howff,
mynd that ye feel superior, unco prood
that coorseness hes been sined oot frae yir harns.

Byt mynd as weill that royal Jamie Fower
wad hae mair in common wi baith leids
not you wi *Beurla Mor* an suddron wards.

An that thare is in baith
a smirr o Scotland that's gane frae yirsel.

Thow hes tynt cultur an yon's an unco loss.

An uair a chailleas neach a mhaoin,
Is gnothach faoin bhith ag iarraidh mios. [32]

Is it possible to look at Scotland soberly,
a knuckle-end of rock upon a boulder
spinning through infinity.
Perhaps the love of country is only like
supporting a football team, a tribe, extended family.
Surely all men but fools consider this?

But time and again we are betrayed
not by our instinct but the *practical*
idea that only what is useful matters.
Market Forces are the ultimate moral sanction
in beehive or anthill: those who bargain best
are those who deserve survival, clear the glens
so dwellers in the far cities get cheap mutton.
The clansmen died to make them warmer gansays.
The Hucksters always win, float to the top
of mankind's soup, and then what's *useful* changes.
The sheep depart, deer-stalker and bird-slaughterer
walk in the wilderness. The people go
from blackhouse to city slum. But this is hardly
to maximise the pleasure of the most.

Where then is *country, nation*
the New Jerusalem you sing about so proudly
in London's privileged halls?
Part of it must be in your slum cities
far from the shouting maniacs of your markets,
the ten years frenzied yelling in the City,
burned-out useless retirement to stockbroker Tudor
or poverty once again.

The only true totem of *Englishness* lies in language:
Chaucer, Gawaine, Shakespeare, Hardy, Dickens,
not measurable in economic terms.

Deutschland ist über alles in the works
of Goethe, Schiller, Beethoven and Heine
held in the head. It has no scope
in dreams of *Herrenvolk* or *Lebensraum*.

The glory that was Greece lives on in words,
Stranger, tell the Spartans that here we lie,
obedient to their orders: only Simonides
reflects the valour that was Lacedaemon.
Poquelin did more for France that Bonaparte.

Likewise, I tell you, Scotland lives in words:
if you care nothing for the speech of Scots,
Scotland is lost to you: elsewhere are hills as high
rivers as long and deep and fields as green.

The Isles of Greece were bright in Byron's eye
as Lochnagar. The mountains look on Marathon
but now the galleys grapple in Herodotus:
the ships and men are mouldered down by time.
Zoe mou, sas agapo: Greece lives in Byron's word.

Tir gun chanan, tir gun anam
A tongueless land's a land without a soul:
a land that has no spirit.

A poet should approve of every tongue,
strive in his verse to swell the hoard of words
know of the poets who walked the land before him.

All beauty is enhanced by multiformity:
No apple's won when all are Aphrodite.
All poetry's barren when one word is banned.
Only the foolish damn what they cannot read.

Better than words is the great silence,
For stillness is the realm of holiness.

But silence is for sainthood, not for poetry,
The *muthos* of a people lies in words.

Sae I will sai: *O freedom is a noble thing*
freedom makes man to have liking
and these are *Scottish words*
unknown to Scots, it seems,
as are the words of Finlay
sounding across the years:

Sgrìobh go fiosach fìreòlach
a seanchas is a gcaithrèim;
nà beir duan air mhìsheòladh
go a lèigheadh go Mac Cailèin. [33]

---

1   *MacCailein*...here translated as Great Colin, was the earl of Argyll who at that
    time was very pro-Scottish and pro-Gaelic. This is a translation of the Gaelic
    which follows it.

2   The stanza is by Fionnlaigh Mac an Aba from the *Book of the Dean of Lismore*.
    It starts with satirical comment about strolling poets and ends with a injunction
    to foster Scotland's culture and history. A paraphrase in English follows some
    lines further on.

3   What is wrong with Scotlandshire/especially amongst our modern bard are ques-
    tions like: 'who will read my song?'/or 'What language and who will understand
    it? and but for a scarce and honourable few/pour ceaseless contempt on the tongue
    of their ancestors.

4   Wattie, Will, Rab: Walter Kennedy, William Dunber, Robert Henryson.

5   George Campbell Hay

6   Old Gaelic prosodic metres

7   There is many a foolish babbling/sitting in ahigh chair (or the 'city') prating of the beauties of our Gaelic poetry/and will learn no word of it./People who value externals only: Clan this and Clan that and Clan Down-with-the-Gaelic/with the Buggins or Noggins tartans round their arses.

8   The makers of 'Mouth music'.

9   Horee horo my nut brown maid/I never will go North again/I'll sing no song on Iona/the sound fo the pipes will not quickly lift my spirit.

10   And many a verse yet can be heard in the Western Isles/and new poetry appearing from youngsters and old folk.

11   Welsh. 'The Man of the North'. The Cymric chieftains of pre-Gealic Scotland who went south to found a dynasty in Wales.

12   Freely adapted from Alasdair MacDonald's Gaelic poem in praise of the Gaelic language (fl. 1700-1770)

13   Alleged variant spelling of 'Shakespeare'.

14   dagreu/dakrua (tears) and buachaill/buokolos (herdsmen) are Welsh and Gaelic words with close Greek cognates.

15   my thousand curses

16   Adapted from a foreword to *Fontamara* by Ignazio Silone.

17   The first line is from the modern Italian poet Giuseppe Bellosi. The second is a standard Italian rendition by Loris Rambelli. The third is the English translation. The Swiss-German lines are by Johann Hebel (1760-1826) a clergyman, and the Scots and Gaelic echo his words: 'I take pleasure in all these things and refresh my heart with all the scents and beauty'.

18   Alas, I get no respite/trying in my own verse/to get three tongues to pull on one oar/a thing not fashionable in our generation.

19   And our oldest language, sad Gaelic/gets off by the skin of its teeth today/in spite of much spite and wounding/long may she live/language of our first fame.

20   Refers to Walter Kennedy (b. Maybole, Abderseenshire c1460). The following line is William Dunbar's. Ualraig is claimed as the ancestor of that family and the name survives in Carrick and Galloway as MacGoldrick. Carrick was then Gaelic-speaking.

21   Kennedy's reply. Scotland was more Scottish, he claims, when 'Irisch' (ie Gaelic) was spoken. This was the tongue of the original Scoti who emigrated from Ireland

to Scotland from the third century onwards. Later (1848) immigrants of the same stock were not so warmly welcomed. Divide and rule sectarianism had arrive. See the lines that follow.

22 Fergus MacErc brought the Scoti from Ireland 3C AD. The 'Tattie Blight' is the famine of the 19th C.

23 Mungo is Kentigern (both Celtic names) and Glasgow is said to mean 'the dear green place'. Welsh and Gaelic variants of saints are often found in Scotland. Ninian and Ringan is another such. Coel Hen was the Cymric ruler from which Kyle district of Ayrshire takes its name.

24 William Livingstone (Uilleam MacDhunleibhe 1808-1870) a Gaelic poet who earned his living as a tailor, was born in Islay and exiled to Tradeston, Glasgow. He knew English, Latin, Greek, Hebrew, French and Welsh.

25 *A message for the Bard*, a poem by Livingston about the Clearances. Translation follows in next stanza.

26 *Whether Highland, my love, or Lowland*, Scotland nourished us. From a poem by George Campbell Hay who wrote fine poetry in Scotland's three tongues.

27 Your frame was not tall/but I saw the giant of your spirit/on the streets of Edinburgh/and green Kintyre in your mind.

28 And if their ears are stopped/by indifference and alien lies/you, George were not to blame./Every year now there are a few gathered on the hill by Hugh's (CNG) Monument/and he worthy of a multitude/But you have no Monument raised to you but your own work/ That is indeed sufficient.

29 After a verse by Rob Donn Mackay's Gaelic poem Song of the Black Coats.

30 The torture of the spirit/most painful in this day/(is) that your country is smothered/under sterility and stupidity/ of each unconsidered opinion/learning is of no value to them/for they have lost the patience/and they save up their speech/since they possess no great store of it./Without Gaelic or Scots they wrestle with London-speak/to put Scottish ideas/into English jackets./They prefer chopped prose/in insoluble puzzles/and if we don't do likewise/we'll be put on the dungheap.

31 And when you see/a poor crofter as work and Gaelic on his tongue/make sure you joke about it/although you don't understand a single word of it/and you'll get the prize of a laugh from clowns with bad English.

32 When wealth is lost, it is useless to seek credit. (Duncan Lothian)

33 See notes 1 and 2

Sawnie's Complaint

(Dan aoireil air an sgath-san nach tuig Gaidhlig no Albais; na's fior-Ghaidheal sibh, gabhaibh mo leisgeul.

A blaud scrievit in heich Inglis fir sic as hace nae grup o the twa aulder leids; gin ye ken ither or baith I'm shair ye'll no tak the strunts.

A Broadsheet in plain English for those who cannot read our other two languages.)

Those bards who used to carp in five-stressed lines
are out of favour in our clever times:
image and sumbol in free verses clashing
put Pope's and Dryden's manner out of fashion.
Wild George, Lord Byron, that reluctant Scot,
gains scanty laurels from this modern lot.
Yet still I'm tempted, when compelled by rage
to crambo-clink out venom by the page:
though rhyming couplets may be out of style
they're much the best mode for satiric bile.
Scots verse or English is another matter...
no traitor I if I should choose the latter,
for modern Scottie had but little knowledge,
(brainwashed in school and then wrung out in college)
of his own tongues; but most can speak and read
(with some small Scottish quirks) the English leid.
Lallans and Erse, alas I must abandon
such English as I have I'll make a stand on.

Bones of dead Picti on Mons Graupius hill
if in those rough-bound something of you still
mingles where skiers on your hard-won heights
learn to appreciate the rich delights
of Scottish hills, Scotch drink and NORTH SEA oil
at which the natives are allowed to toil,
being set from under Scottish nebs to drag
our greedy London master's Scottish swag
while rusting Scottish shipyards beg a tithe
of millions spent ten miles round Rotherhithe...
look on this craggy, rocky knuckle-end
that once you sought in freedom to defend,
now that last vassal of the English race,
our people shameless in their own disgrace.
Your warning stands today, brave Pictish chief...
they make a wilderness and call it peace.

What other land's gulled twice in each decade
by jobbers in the Parliamentary trade
who promise us HOME RULE before elections
quite unashamed by subsequent defections?
These lie to bolster what they call tradition...
to sit by turns in Rule or Opposition,
so deeply sunk in great affairs of state
(that to all nations but their own relate)
unmindful of mean street and bleak hillside
where their constituents miserably bide.
Some pretend Redness, prate of John MacLean
dead long enough to make that safe again;
others, the purest Unionist True Blue
boast PRIVATE ENTERPRISE IS BEST FOR YOU!
when not a TITHE... a THIRD they take away.
'Invest the rest in industry,' they say.
Don't spend the lot on horses, drink and fags...
aspire to riches, Sawnie, from your rags.

Ye hypocrites who from the sale of beer
advance from brewer's tub to ermined peer;
ye statesman who from taxing Indian Weed
pay for the nuclear death ye claim to need;
ye London companies who gorge and swill
the profits from each Scottish whisky still...
pretend that Sawnie's common vices grieve you,
but don't expect a wise man to believe you.

Ye socialists, who plough your private farms,
who far from slumland back in rural charms,
how easily you learn High Tory practice
of subsidising pigs from poor men's taxes.
Sad, honest John MacLean, long laid to rest,
damned by the rich but still by poor men blessed,
owned little land but prison floor and grave.
Enjoy your fields, but don't blaspheme the brave.

Poor Sawnie, he's too dull to see your actions,
but keeps on voting for your tawdrie factions,
and sends you down to London each five years
to further your political careers;
a time for Tweedldum, then Tweedledee:
This year you govern, Dum, then next year me...
Third party interference we can smother
by public fawning over one another,
resolve our pseudo-quarrel for a while
until the errant voters we beguile
by preaching that THREE PARTIES WILL NOT DO!...
we'll win the stray sheep back to me and you.
Then, every time some faction gets together
Dull Taff and Simple Sawnie to deliver,
we'll think up tricks to cover with derision
the thought that they be heard on television;
we'll hit them low in propaganda clinches
by simply starving them of column-inches.

Of course, we needn't feel much apprehension...
trust to the Celtic genius for dissension,
for any group composed of two-score Scots
will soon dissolve to forty different lots:
who's Left, who's Centre, radical or Right...
soon the main issue is forgotten quite...
Thus barren Government and Opposition
preserve a worn-out Cat-and-Dog tradition
forever wrangling in a mock debate...
fake democrats within huckster state.

Fake democrats, you say! Is that quite fair?
Mother of Parliaments, proud name you bear
but seem to favour most those southern sons
who in all battle bear the biggest guns.
Besides, you've found a way of foiling fools:
when things don't suit *your* boys, you change the rules.
A referendum's not one when its bent
to cunning humbug of two-score percent.
Though the whole island sees the count was rotten,
give it a month or so and it's forgotten.

When the day's lost to a true democrat,
Mother of Parliaments, he does not rat
or cheat, or fiddle numbers in a Bill
to foil by Party Tricks the Peoples' Will.
Those who by sharpers' trimming gain their point,
weaken your bones, Old Dame, in every joint.

When Scotland's Parliament, untimely ripped
from Scotland's womb, was south to London shipped,
a carlin who observed the sorry ploy
of this foul closure, said with little joy:
When Scots chiels sate in ben yon Scottish Hoose
and wi oor polity played fast and loose,
stanes roon their heids a Scottish haund micht caa...
but south tae London toun's an unco thraw...

Today, as if to baulk the Scottish will,
we send ambitious placemen Southward still
whose seeking natures thrill with every mile
the night express gains southward of Carlisle,
glad once again to crawl within the womb
of England's dear old mother, Scotland's tomb.
See how they mix there, affable, urbane...
happpy to be in London once again...
discoursing loudly on the World's Affairs
flowing with hope of ministerial chairs.
Quite, quite forgetful of poor Scotland's losses
they tug their forelock to their English bosses.

And Scotland? Once a land in UNION joined,
finds all her ancient privilege purloined;
the worthy pride of an old sturdy nation,
reduced by clowns beneath that honoured station,
while London City Gents, fat on our bounty
equate our Kingdom with an English county.

See in the lounge there, Toombodie MP
who burned to set the Scottish workmen free,
become a trumpet of uncertain sound,
in hopes of office when his turn comes round.
Foul, leaking slums in Scotland, once his care
still leak, and still are foul, and will be there
for him to shout about before elections
and blame them all on Mucklewame's defections.

Mucklewame, champion of Free Enterprise...
visions of ermine grandeur glaze *his* eyes...
in late night queues at Scottish aerodromes
he dreams of long week-ends in stately homes...
of Honours Lists, and how to gain an entry
to permanent acceptance by The Gentry...
while banishing all thoughts of Caledonia

a place (though full of oil) a great deal stonier.
See poor MacCowal, Scotsman to the bone,
eager to serve, who bites his nails at home.
Patriot John Bull's the noblest thing on earth...
but patriot Scots are thought of little worth.

The Scottish name provokes a London sneer.
(All greater Scots, you see, are English there...
Fleming, Clerk Maxwell, Baird or David Hume,
the English pantheon gladly gives them room)
but try to be a *Scottish* politician
who seeks improvement of his land's position...
whispered ill-will soon rises to a roar
while Scottish hirelings rush to swell the score.
For True Democracy, it seems is not
allowed as birthright to the decent Scot.

'Each to his own' would seem an honest quote
but England keeps her hand round Scotland's throat;
while Scotland rots and bleeds her wealth and brains
her idiot offspring sing North British strains:
mean 'kenned-his-faither' numbskulls swank and stump
their brainless envy round each parish pump...
such Scots as ponder on the Scottish name
slink to the hills, or drink to hide their shame.

The rest, to London bound in drunken batches,
bawl out their patriot zeal at football matches,
suck sweets and read historical romances
or prance in too-long kilts in country dances;
deer-stalking dunces crawl through heather clumps
past shattered pulp-mills, weed-grown smelter-dumps...
Tweed-skirted dames, shod with expensive brogues,
sell home-made jam to purchase votes for rogues:
while lounge-bar lefties, dressed to fit the role
mouth dialectic to confound the prole.

At Conference the clay-foot statesmen mention
Planned Devolution that they've no intention
(once sat in Westminster) of ever ceding,
since after all, they're likely to be needing
our heather acres till the oil runs dry...
or they arrange our nuclear Goodbye.

Crionadh Foghlam na h-Alba

The Crynan o Scotia's Lear

The Decline of Scottish Learning

(Dan Macaronach Le Foclair Agus Eadar-Theangachadh
Ae Macaronic Ballant wi Glossarie and Owresettan
A Macaronic Ballad with Glossary and Translation)

'Sgriobh gu Fiosach Fìreòlach a Sheanchas is a gCaithrèim'
Fionnlagh Mac an Aba c.1500

1   After the tumult and the shouting died
    under the vaulted ceilings of Dunedin
    where vain and empty heads had swooned and sighed
    on ploughman-bards who showed such noble breeding,
    you chose auld claes and parritch in the west.
    That for our sakes, was surely for the best.

2   Hired to the Whigamores, uneasy pax
    you tholed, and scribbled in a Doon-Hame vennel;
    collected the hated Hanoverian tax
    up to your fecket in the Solway channel.
    Wherever your heart was, Rab, it was not here
    chasing stags of the soul in gauger's gear.

3   Now, annually, some pan-loaf speaking ass
    gives a few ill-learned lines of yours the air
    seeks with an empty speech to bring to pass
    Scotland's resurgences for three hours a year,
    while big-wamed Baillies bawl out 'Scotland Yet',
    till the bleak dawn, when jaded minds are set

4   to the prudent task of keeping the balance right;
all Scotchness fettered in a toadie's heart
in a land that smothers under bad advice...
first-fruits of London's governmental art,
for Mr Sunday-Scotland your new MP
whose party place outbids democracy.

5   Our Scottish leids are openly despised;
in bookish cliques there's no debate upon
what tongue will best achieve the Glittering Prize:
concord of London critic, Oxbridge don.
Gaelic and Scots the *maestri* now omit
from New Licht seminars on 'Scottish' Lit.

6   There's chiels that scrieve in Scots baith real an Plastic
some read the ane an blether in the ither;
a wheen micht gie ye Gaelic gin ye ask it
or Beurla Mor withooten muckle bother.
But whaur the 'Scottish' literati gether
its seenil ye'll hear ocht but Inglis cletter.

7   Agus an diugh, ged is gle bhochd ar saoghal
tha Ruaraidh againn agus Somhairle Mor
a sgriobhas *lingua Scotorum* le gaol
an teanga 'thuirt an Cinneideach bu choir
a bhith aig gach fìor-Albannach mar chainnt:
am measg na graisge sud is beag an t-seans.

8   An gentil skeelie Deorsa mac Iain Deors'
nou ane wi Alasdair an Duncan Ban
scrievit in three leids wi an eident force
fir sic-like Scots as in three leids kin scan.
Dh'innis e dhuinn: *'son airgead no ni...
na treig do thalamh dhuthchais'*...ochan i!

9   Nou that great Mac a' Greidhir's in the box
    (hou monie ken the Gaelic fir his name?)
    the fleggit aidders slide oot frae the rock
    tae set aboot their Scotland-smoorin game
    turn Cockney cac-nam-bo oot by the quair
    tae cheinge auld Alba intil Scotlandshire.

10   It sud rise birses when some London scunner
    tellied tae ilka Scottish but-an-ben
    caa's ye PROVINCIAL! Some wee southran wunner
    blethran o Kultur efter News at Ten.
    We maun be scrieving literate defiance
    no snirtain in a cultural compliance.

11   Mac Mhaighstir Alasdair abandoned school,
    threw off the scholar's gown for belted tartan,
    supporting not so much princely fool
    as a more desperate cause he'd set his heart on
    (how difficult for some the honest thought
    that Scotland should be governed by the Scot.)

12   And skulking back at last when all was over
    to bitter lurking in Dunedin's streets,
    he managed still such spirit to recover
    as made new songs to fit poor Scotland's needs.
    But Sons of Scotlandshire, to our great loss
    burned his new verses at the Mercat Cross.

13   A process that still works for them you'll find
    for Scots and Gaelic writing find no other
    echo within the dull North British mind
    than a mere envious desire to smother
    all that's most Scottish in this dowie land.
    Our sad dead bards look on a weary band...

14 of poetasting dunces whose intention
    (guided by what's the fashion in the South)
    bows only to what southern critics mention.
    the *filid* down at heel and down at mouth
    write their wersh lines in gurlie native jargon
    to help them thole the miserable bargain.

15 Gif London's approbation's aa they want
    oor Scottish leids til Grub Street canna help thaim,
    let cultural ken-better gaup and gaunt,
    in crambo-clinkan duans I maun skelp thaim,
    raxin oot whiles tae grup ane by the hauch
    and dreg his grunzie frae yon fremit trouch.

16 If, unregairdit, Scotland's leids maun perish,
    by misbehadden learlessness coost doon,
    yon southran souch thet they sae muckle cherish
    wull et the lest oor native mainners droon.
    Let aa they Scrieve by wyce and gleg and modish,
    there's ae thing siccar, it wull no be Scottish.

NOTES

The two Gaelic lines by Finlay MacNab are 'Write knowledgeably and with true
learning of their history and culture.'

2 That Burns was a Jacobite sympathiser is obvious from his poetry and correspon-
   dance.

6 Plastic Scots: the kind of universal and historical mixture of Scots used by
   MacDiarmid.

Another Letter to Lord Byron

(Readers will recall that Byron was so aroused to fury by a review in the Edinburgh Review of March 1808 that he wrote a satiric diatribe against Scotsh reviewers in general and Jeffrey the editor in particular, and damned in his verses all those whom the Edinburgh Reviewers praised. It is often forgotten that Byron himself once pointed out that he had been born half a Scot and bred a whole one. It will also be remembered that W. H. Auden whiled away some of his time in Iceland writing a Letter to Lord Byron. Writing letters to phantoms may be as vain an occupation in all senses of the word as publishing Broadsheets. The only possible excuse is that a third party will be amused.)

If from the slopes of some remote Parnassus
you deign to look upon this mortal coil
whereon our modern insolence surpasses
the dead conceits that brought you to the boil...
forgive me if I burn the midnight oil
converted by the Electricity Board
who've made it cheaper, though the price has soared,

to write you, George, (I lay aside the title,
and call you George, or maybe Mister Gordon)
I feel that Scottish surname's somehow vital
when Scotland's quirks I'm keeping watch and ward on...
I know such antics make you yawn with boredom...
You may well ask me how I have the face to,
but I don't know who else to put my case to.

'Born half a Scot,' you said, 'and bred a whole one...'
Harrow and Cambridge smothered out the Scot...
a process that has ceased now to appal one...
the commmon practice of our posher lot...
whether their land's heredit'ry or bought,
against our thistly ways they take precaution
and send their scions southward for brainwashing.

Of course your Scottish chromosones still rankled
just like my own (though maybe not with pride)
since with our Scotch reviewers once you tangled
when they had given your stuff a bumpy ride;
but whether critics praise you or deride...
its better far they should provoke your rages
than send back manuscripts and slight your pages.

I share with you, I must confess the fault,
a certain penchant for sardonic stanzas
that throw an acid literary salt
among those delicate extravaganzas
that get in print; prosodian Sancho Panzas
to show that windmills rarely giants frame...
or windbag scribblers, for that's just the same.

I've read your howls of anger and frustration
when northern critics fuelled your distresses.
At least you had achieved some publication;
Proud Scotland then possessed some printing presses.
Now though some inky saints remain to bless us...
grey Edimbro the large founts all abandon,
and with all other trimmers flee to London.

I live upon a distant western moor
where Gaelic names adorn both farm and mountain;
heather, not roses, grow around my door,
the loch's my spring, not far Castalia's fountain...
you'll hear the grouse whirr, see the roe deer bounding,
hear the sheep bleat, the shaggy cattle bellow,
but seldom meet a literary fellow.

Forgive me, Mister Gordon, a frustration
that makes me scribble to your wispy ghost;
a crank who still regards the Scottish Nation
as still extant, though very nearly lost...
some think it merest history, at most.
Clever chaps find me (don't you think it sad)
a scoundrel patriot – gone slightly mad.

The country's full of nineteenth centuries Tories
(though Fabian Socialists are still around)
our dear old Liberals tell the ancient stories
to bore me with Westminster's hollow sound.
Every four years they cover the same ground,
impervious to yawns and snores and sighs
they deafen Scotland with the same old lies.

So leave the politics to politicians...
since statesmen show once in a thousand years;
let fools bask in Utopian superstitions
and smother Hansard in their boos and cheers...
we buy their steaks and subsidise their beers,
but whether sour or lyric, bland or mordant...
we both think versifying more important.

Some Scottish scribblers indicate direction,
leave them to swing, their noses all point south,
since west and north they think have predilections
for strange old words that rumble in the mouth
and sound barbaric, weird, arcane, uncouth...
the Great Plook does not like these very much
preferring Oxbridge-Fleet-Street prose and such.

From time to time I have to look for reasons
why Scotchness I should think of such import...
when I myself might take up those same treasons
adopted by the southward-seeking sort;
aim at the kind of English heard at court...
paint Sawnie as a flag-day Aberdonian
and damn the guts of all thing Caledonian.

My Lord, when you'd won south from Aberdeen
despite those verses on Dark Lochnagar...
back home in Scotland you were seldom seen
where all those Calvanistic bogies are...
One touch of Scotchness may from fame debar;
the literary list-compiling lot
rarely point out that you were half a Scot.

But then, why should they? If you're good enough
to gain the ear of the great word outside
they'll make you English....cockney-fy your stuff
like David Hume; gulp down all Scottish pride
you'll gain a reputation far and wide.
Damn Scottishness! accept the English order...
you never need look back across the Border.

There, George, I'm off again both stern and wild
perfervidum ingenium and all that...
but is this really patriotism or bile?
Scotch cockernonie or a Luton hat,
or wreath of laurel on the forehead sat...
toga or Gaulish cloak or philabeg,
are bards not bards in socked or buskined leg?

The SCOTSMAN's filled with letters every day...
indignant over England's usurpation,
where each one points out his own private way...
how to escape from southern domination.
I must confess, not without some elation
I watch these mangy Scottish birses rise.
It brings, at times, salt tears into my eyes.

What is this Scottishness they love so much?
They don't like bishops, only moderators...
though when have bishoprics and such
our poor old nation had a better status.
Are we held up on Calvin's cold afflatus?
Did not the Butcher burn the *Piskie* steeple,
lock up *their* ministers, and hang *their* people? [1]

Or else they say: we have the Scottish Law
(only judiciary, there's no legislature)
and think this gives them some great cause to crow...
it gives the place a more official nature.
But when *The Eagle* sank upon *The Creatures* [2]
of English Admirals they asked permission
before they dared set up a Scotch Commission.

Some say, my Lord: at least we have our language...
I wonder, now what language do they mean?
Our plebs pronounce a sandwich *sangwich*...
does this from Englishness divorce them clean?
Scots they think common, Gaelic's seldom seen,
save when its daubed on traffic signs by CEARTAS... [3]
even there the crafty Cambrians outsmart us.

Of course at threescore I'm a bit oldfashioned
with rhyming diatribes that nearly scan;
my whole sour soul with Scottishness impassioned...
a trait fastidious poetasters damn.
Sometimes I nearly rhyme, like metric psalms...
there's no old trick that in my verse is stinted...
which makes it difficult to get them printed.

Some say my stuff's a bit like tinker piping...
all on one tune, a fault I will confess to;
I'm thirled to bitter Caledonian griping...
a broadsheet bullying in the end addressed to
converts; although I know it would be best to
abandon rhymes like this and court Euterpe.
(The rhymes for her are rather less than thirty)

Last night I read a life of Robert Burns...
for all his faults I still admire the fellow...
polemicising Scot, and bard by turns
from sweet song o the patriotic bellow...

a trait that hard experience failed to mellow.
Goaded by fools and patonised by snobs
and forced by failing crops to sue for jobs.

How did he manage to maintain the stance
of Scottishness in life and of the work?
'Don't write in Scots' they said, 'you won't advance...
They'll read you no more than they would a Turk.
Eschew such sords and *crannreuch*, *blate* and *mirk*
stell, *sheuch* and *scunner* score out from your list;
say: hold and ditch and frost and sky and mist.

I know, my Lord, you hated Scotch Reviewers.
Hydra, I think you called them in your spleen;
the lines they praised you thought fit for the sewers;
those bards whose feathers Jeffrey chose to preen
not to be heard, you held, or even seen
in hard black print on any decent page.
And yet I sigh for that Athenian age...

When bards in Southwell were so stung to ire
by publishers upon the Canongate,
as wish to roast them in satiric fire;
could we but find again that blessed state
when English bards on Scotch opinion wait;
when scrribblers paid such earnest close attention
to anything in Scotland worth a mention.

Is anything in Scotland worth a mention?
Where Fleet Street rules and London presses rumble
to southern tastes all scribes must pay attention
to see the bright coins through their fingers tumble.
Poor Simple Sawnie really mustn't grumble
if when a laureate bard they must appoint...
all Scottish noses are put out of joint.

Grecian Lord Byron, is it not unjust,
that scribblers living close to Piccadilly
now that our native printing presses rust,
should think our land barbarian, hairy, hilly
tartan-and-whiskified and cold and silly...
object to native words like *theek* and *thole* ⁴
because *they* did not hear them when at school?

A few bold warriors at their ledgers squinting
in hope the black will just outscore the red
go in for risks like publishing and printing
such lines as boom within the Scottish head.
Perfervidum ingenium, nearly dead,
from brave small presses gets an upward hitch...
but patriot poetry-printers don't get rich.

Even the stuff *you* wrote that rhymed and scanned
won't do in London now; your bold Don Juan
from the London lists would certainly be banned
and like the rest of us you'd face black ruin.
For clear-as-day type bards there's nothing doing
if you've no bent for crossword-clue obscurity
an ear for form and content are no surety

against the talentless, the dreary dunce
who knows no prosody and makes no sense
but haunts each London literary lunch,
wagging a sheaf of verses, dull and dense
and looking interesting, strung out and tense;
if once he gets some pundit to protect him
the editors are frightened to reject him.

So then, my Lord, hater of Scottish presses,
of Scotch reviewers, northern criticasters...
mark well the Scotch scribbler's new distresses
now Grub Street dribblers have become our masters.
Greater by far, Lord George, are our disasters
than any long-dead Edinburgh Review
which failed to give you what you thought your due.

That's it, my Lord. To finish I'll make haste.
Your ghost, I'm sure must be much madder still
to know the arbiters of every taste
live in that five-mile-stews round Ludgate Hill.
Should Jeffrey's thin wraith skulk behind you still
he'll grin and smirk to see you get the blues
now London writes, prints, reads mere Parish News.

[1]   See *The Scottish Church and Nation* Donaldson G.

[2]   *The Iolaire* (Gael. eagle) sank on the Beasts of Holm on January 1 1919. Many Lewis men who survived the Great War were lost.

[3]   Justice. A body dedicated to the obtaining of official status for Gaelic.

[4]   thole, was objected to by a London critic as archaic.

The Jolly Trimmers

or

Love of Slavery

A Satirical Cantata

(In sad memory of, and with apologies to, that great bard, rebel and true Scot, Robert Burns)

Recitativo

When Januar crannreuch bites the taes
and bodies seek the ingle's bleeze
or some mair modern lowe;
when warmit howffs are socht oot maist
and toddie's mair tae ilka taste
tae wames baith cauld and howe...
sic nichts when blests of Januar wun
remind us aw o Rabbie
an set the bardic saul tae spin
oot dauds o Standard Habbie;
wi tatties, an haggis
richt found fur usquebae
the thrissle, maun rissle
fur three hours on yae day.

Sic nichts ye'll find the Suppers stert,
the last dunt o the Scottish hert
aw smoort by London capers;
whaur honest chiels are aw gart think
and ithers come juist fur the drink
or hope tae mak The Papers.
Tis there ye'll see amang the rest,
in siller studs and laces,
Big Mucklewame in tartans drest,
amang yon sonsie faces;
we speechin, and preachin
his view o Scotland's State,
he'll tell ye, an sell ye
gin ye wad tak his bait.

Big Mucklewames Song

A son of Mammon I and I tell you all no lie...
for I could sell and buy every man in the room;
but I'll never be content with a grain of ten percent
and I bolster up the rent of each roof that I own.

Chorus: Lal de daudle etc...

And although I made my pile between Kirkwall and Carlisle
its many a long mile that I've left them behind;
I've a house in London Town and another further down
where the southern social graces are more to my mind.

Where to further suit my ends I have made a lot of friends
for a pile of money tends to attract a bunch,
and I whisper to them words on the subject of The Lords
when they're round my festive board I treat them to lunch.

Our dear old Robert Burns, well enough he served our turns
and our great respect he earns for his verses of note:
we make Scottish noises here at the dead time of the year
but we really have no fear when it comes to the vote.

We can plumb the Scottish deeps with the haggis and the neaps
for we're certain that it keeps down all Scottish desires;
as a safety valve its best, for all sep'ratist unrest...
and for me an annual test of our dear Scotlandshire.

Recitativo

He endit tae a roosan cheer
and stampin on the flair...
and aw his freens wha'd cam tae hear
nou yelloched oot fur mair;
but Lady Mucklewame wis near
tae quaiten doun the rair...
aw glitterin in her West End gear
she shovit back her chair.

Lady Mucklewame's Song

My Dad was a climber, my Dad was no fool
for he paid all my fees to the Very Best School,
while I had good advice for both Mumsie and Daddie
to walk up the aisle with a well-heeled laddie.

Dear Mumsie made sure that I 'came out' in Town
in the hope that I'd catch some baronial clown,
but if chinless was tinless I'd never go steady
but look all around for a well-heeled laddie.

The very first cast hooked a penniless peer
who sponged on his title for most of the year;
but those who prize sturgeon above finnan haddie
must set home the gaff in a well-heeled laddie.

So despite the blue ichor that ran in his veins
I dumped my lean Duke for more affluent swains;
to rule his new Scottish estate I was ready,
so I tilted my cap at the Mucklewame laddie.

Now gillies and stalkers I have by the score,
for in the far north I find game birds galore
and bowers and scrapers to call me My Lady
in hopes of a smile from my well-heeled laddie.

So on our way Northwards we take it in turns
to pretend we love tartan and haggis and Burns...
a poet who never had much of the ready...
I'm much better off with my well-heeled laddie.

Recitativo

Toombodie gled tae get a bite
sat guzzlin et a lower table,
wi usquebae bambaizilt quite
as muckle o't as he was able
fair tozie wi a guid nicht's soakin
he thocht as weel tae gie a sang
nou that he didna care a docken
fur the graund folk he sate amang.

Toombodie's Song

Auld Scotia's the land o my birth
Auld Scotland's the name o my nation;
though I've daunnert across the wide Earth
I never hae felt sic frustration,
as when I cam back tae my hame
an saw whit the fowk there had made o't
a kintra that's no worth the name
that my noble forefathers yince laid on't.
Braid Scots was the leid that I spak
on the day that I left the dockside;
in Gaelic I learnt how tae crack
when I leeved my auld mither beside.

But nou its become Scotland*sheer*
(fur yon is the wey they pronounce it)
there's nae ither leid that I hear
than 'pan-loaf' and I hereby renounce it;
now they tak the auld leids frae the bairns
in the interests of standardisation…
fur the elders they aw lackt the harns
that formerly marked oot the nation.

But wha is there wad listen tae me
wha speak the auld leids o the land;
fur they arna the tongue o TV
or yon Oxbridge-cum-Westminster band.

An nou ilka speug that I hear
cheepin oot in oor high public places…
Ah, Rabbie, Ye're faur batter there,
whaur ye're lowsit fra sic airs and graces.

Recitativo

Tae claim their lugs cam neist a lady
in tartan sash and Heilant cadie
nae crofter wes her husband's daddie
but fain he'd be a Heiland laddie;
Though Eton was his Alma Mater
he'd got ten million frae his pater,
and sae wi attitudes colonial
he chieftain'd it in Scotch Baronial.

The Song of the New Laird's Lady

A highland chief my love would be...
the fashion in Society;
he purchased to impress his friend
a fortress in the lonely glens.

Chorus:
Sing hey my new John Heilandman
Sing ho my new John Heilandman
For London Glossies now they stand
and pose round my John Heilandman.

Wi private tartan kilt an plaid
in Edinboro neatly made,
he makes wee birdies fear the gun
o my synthetic Heilandman.

Though west of Spey and north of Forth
of Heiland laddies there's a dearth,
these empty spaces suit the plan
of such as my John Heilandman.

They say they went across the sea
and left the place to John and me;
for miles and miles the moors you'll scan
and scarcely see a Highlandman.

But on the Twelfth the local poor
creep out from cairns to beat the moor
though Gaelic chatter then we ban...
it much annoys my Heilandman. [1]

And after all the birds are shot
the London gourmets eat the lots;
the moor's deserted once again
for me and my John Heilandman.

Recitativo

Straucht up there stood a pigmy pedant
wha et nit-pickin skeels was eident
he could bambaizle ilka bejant
wi's share of lear,
't was aw his walth and he wes gled on't
and gart thaim hear...

Wi een fast shut and finger raisit
ilk southron scribblers wark he praisit
while his puir bejants blate and dazit
soaked up his sermon;
the native wark he thocht debasit...
their scrievers vermin.

The Pedant's Song

Tho bred tae speak the Scottish tongue
I smoort it oot when I wes young
but whether spoken wards or sung
I whustle owre the lave o't.

I am a pedant tae my trade.
tho Scottish born I'm southron made;
what if a traitor game I've played
I whustle owre the lave o't.

In lectures and in seminars
at parties or in city bars,
I find the Scottish language jars
and whustle owre the lave o't.

O coorse, the bardies o the past,
deep in their lang-hame yirdit fast
o thaim I shaw my learning vast
but whustle owre the lave o't.

Recitativo

At yon a sturdy artisan
wha's got an invitation
fur gien the Club a helpin hand
(tho faur abune his station)
the pedant heized by the lapel
an thocht it richt tae heid him...
syne that the way he spak himsel
wes as his forbears gied him.

The pedant made shift tae appease
this king o square and level
and said he had but tried tae please
the ithers in the revel.
He winked his ee aboot the ring
and said the man was fleein
when up the calllant raise tae sing
in accents maist plebeian.

The Journeyman's Song

My maisters aw, sae bien and braw,
I am a bonie worker,
wi bolt or nail I never fail
tae shaw I am nae shirker;
I've sairved my time in monie a clime
an airned my keep richt brawlie
but nou I'm hame I win nae fame
whaur sma men aye misca me.

Wi my ain nieve ma skeel I'll preive
gin ye'll pit wark afore me;
yince, ilka tide upon the Clyde
there's no a man could waur me
yince, Scottish maisters fee'd my haund
an peyed me Scottish siller
but I maun seek some fremit land
when London hauds the tiller.

Recitativo

Anither had been listin there
but silent at his cup;
wha cam tae be at this affair
in hopes of bite and sup:
weel read in aw his kintra's lear
baith leids o't in his grup
no gart by favour or by fear
he thocht tae steer thaim up
wi's sang that nicht.

Frae Deorsa til the Book o Deer [2]
frae Hughie til the Dean [3]
there was nae word o Scottish lear
but that oor bard had seen;
weel could he thole the bitter sneer
the jag o envie's preen;
frae siccan chiels as didna care
tae tak a Scottish lean,
in sang that nicht.

Tho critics seenil sang his praise
an rare his publication,
the Scottish saul he saucht tae raise
tae pride in our auld nation.
He wisna like tae take the bays
for siccan exhortation,
nou Scotland does as England says
withooten altercation.
Ilk day and nicht.

The Bard's Song

There's nane regard me as bard
in smairt reviews AND aw that;
braid Scots or Erse houever terse
it's doggerel thay ca that

Chorus
For aw that and aw that
In English Lit. and aw that,
they'd raither chance a Pink Romance
than ocht in Scots and aw that

The 'in-crowd' bank in serried rank
fur Gaelic bards and aw that,
but whether damns they hear or psalms
they've nae idea fur aw that.

Tho Chaucer's strains they teach the weans
the southron bards and aw that,
puir Henryson will no get dune,
he's ower Scotch fur aw that.

Oor guid braid Scots, suburban lots
will caa it 'slang' and aw that:
an dominies will tak their fees
fur German, French and aw that.

When Jaik and Jill depairt the schuil
they yaise sic lear and aw that
for Moliere beside the fire
and Holderlin an aw that.

An yince a year (nae mair I fear)
in Scottish schools it's law that
the weans tak turns reciting Burns...
neist day they maunna daur that.

Recitativo

Sae sang the bard an in the room
the listeners were stricken doom
and kent ne whit tae dae;
twa that were there, weel fed and beered
the rebel bard wad fain have cheered
gin yin had shawn the wey.
But maist of thaim luikt et their plate
tae hide their lowin chafts
frae yin wha nither bauch nor blate
had lowsed at thaim sic shafts.
He rising, surprised them
wi words baith bauld and braisant
a joyful disciple
o yon great Ayrshire peasant.

The Poet's Finale

Who believe the Scottish nation
is of old and noble seed;
must with others take up station
equal but no 'lesser breed'.

Chorus
All around the trimmers coax you
to despise a Scottish stance
all around the placemen hoax you
lead you in their party dance.

Some for wealth and some for title
some for place or private plan
would your natuce insticts bridle,
mould you to a lesser man.

Listen to our native voices
faint enough though they may be;
you'll be offered louder choices
fading when they've made you pay.

Cast an eye round moor and city
in our dowie Scottish land;
slum and larach get no pity
Scottie's robbed on every hand.

The daftest bairn knows rule by strangers
smothers out the native will;
family firms have lesser dangers,
family fingers in the till.

Night and day the trimmers wangle
add, subtract, the placemen know
how to cover every angle,
keep daft Scottie down below.

Chorus
All around the trimmers coax you
to despise a Scottish stance;
all around the placemen hoax you
lead you in their party dance.

---

[1] Beaters were sometimes reproved for speaking Gaelic.

[2] The by-name of the late George Campbell Hay. *The Book of Deer* is the earliest
   Scots Gaelic document.

[3] A collection of Gaelic poetry compiled in the sixteenth century.

On Satire, Mavericks and Scotland: William Neill in conversation with Gerry Cambridge

WILLIAM NEILL WAS BORN IN 1922 IN PRESTWICK, AYRSHIRE, where his father was the owner of a small hotel. He was educated at Ayr Academy and, many years later, at Edinburgh University as a mature student, where he took an Honours degree in Celtic and English studies. In the interim years, he served in the Air Force. He is the only living Scottish poet fully conversant with Scotland's three languages: Gaelic, Scots and English, to give them, as he would say, their proper order of seniority. This interview was conducted in the kitchen of the Galloway home he shares with his wife Dodo, and was frequently punctuated by Neill's laughter and by Dodo's asides. In person, Neill is far from the cantankerous poet of repute, but genial, witty and possessing an encyclopaedic knowledge of matters Scottish and poetic.

GERRY CAMBRIDGE: When I think of you in relation to Scottish poetry, I align you with people like MacDiarmid, Tom Scott and so on – mavericks.

WILLIAM NEILL: Oh, I feel a great affinity with mavericks. After all, if people are mavericks, they must be getting near some kind of originality. If they're not mavericks, they're in the swim. They've got all their pals telling them what it's best to do. Mavericks do their own thing, like Crabbe, John Clare, Blake: the great originals.

GC: Does the poetry world need its mavericks?

WN: Yes indeed. The mavericks of course don't feel good about being mavericks all the time, because you don't want to be ignored: it's difficult to be a maverick and popular. You get no mentions, you get no reviews, people look down their noses. Most of the Scottish poets have been, to some extent, mavericks. You're almost forced into being a maverick if you're a Scottish poet. Most Scots who are poets, to put it mathematically, also happen to live in the country; so they become mavericks by virtue of distance and separation.

GC: That may be true of some of the older generation of poets; but most of the younger poets have urban backgrounds. Few of them are notably pastoral writers.

WN: True, but then you don't get many people left who know anything about the older Scotland. This is one of the things that worries me. For instance you get people talking about 'Scotland' on the television who quite plainly don't know anything about it. They make colossal historical errors, errors of language, and they go along with London views of everything. London has an influence out of all proportion to its worth. If it's the London view, it's accepted without question. This is one of the things I find almost intolerable: the fact that people get jobs in Scotland as editors, and they come straight from London, and know nothing about the Scots, Scottish language or history; yet they're praised to the skies. Why is this? People who really know about Scotland linguistically, historically, and in every other way, are ignored; nobody listens to them.

GC: One of your satires is called 'The Jolly Trimmers'. It deals with some of the themes you've just enumerated. Few poets seem to write satires any more. Why do you think that is?

WN: Fear. You get into trouble for writing satire. Gaelic poets who wrote satire were hunted out of the clan, and hunted all over the place. The Roman satirists such as Juvenal weren't at all popular. Yet there's a need for satire. People have to write satire in order that the satirised can have a good look at themselves. I think of Belli for instance. Splendid satire, about the

Roman worthies. Garie [Robert Gairioch] has translations of Belli which delighted me. You know the one about the fellow walking home and being knocked down by a coach; this wee chick sittin in the coach says 'wha dees, dees; drive on' (laughter). Belli really hits the nail on the head as regards Roman society: the grandees at the top and the *hoi polloi* at the bottom. And Belli knew them all, had come from the top to the bottom and gone back to the middle, and really had seen them all. Every nation in the world has had satire. But not many satirists get on very well until they're dead. Pope for instance.

GC: So satire will still be being written, but not being seen.

WN: True. But if you have satire in your bones, you can't stop writing it. And there are people left who value it. I recently had a book reviewed in a thesis, in an Italian University, by a person who obviously appreciates that I write satire, and believes that the satire is what gives force to my work. When I stop writing satire I feel dead in some way. You have to have a personality that makes you read the newspaper and roar out in rage. Most people don't have that reaction. Cartoonists have probably taken the place of poets as far as satire goes. I think you really have to feel it. I write a lot of satire about people who are in high places with, in my view, no justification for it. There's not much I can do about this, I'm not destined to get into these high places. There may be a kind of jealousy in this, or a kind of envy, but the only way I can get even, as the Yanks put it, is through satire, and hope that somebody reads it.

GC: Burns, with whom you have certain affinities, was a great satirist.

WN: To me, 'Holy Willie's Prayer' is the best piece of poetry ever written by Burns. It's absolutely scathing, and funny. Nowadays, one of the things you daren't be is funny. If you're funny, you're not a serious poet, you see. Poets all go around in black cloaks and clogs, with wide hats and glum faces. If they're not being taken seriously as poets, they're not poets. This is bunkum of course, but it's a popular modern view. You have to have a long face.

GC: Where does that idea come from?

WN: It's the idea of being serious. If you're serious you're special. A great deal of modern poetry is considered to be the distillation of essences. This to me is bunkum. You don't deliberately go out for a walk and think *I must find an essence this afternoon*. Burns thinks of Holy Wullie himself, walks into the pub, and recites it to his pals. One of the things I admire about Burns is that in the midst of this diatribe Willie Fisher, Holy Wullie himself, walks into the pub, and Burns doesn't stop reading it. He wasn't always a man of principle, but in that case he was.

GC: Where was that?

WN: In Mauchline. There's an Ayr-Dumfries thing about Burns. If you're born in Ayr, you say that Ayrshire gave Burns birth and Dumfries kilt [killed] him; if you're born in Dumfries, you say Ayr drove him oot and Dumfries gave him a livin. Burns was a many-faceted man who had good cause to write satire about the people he dealt with. I'm surprised he never wrote any satire about Friar's Carse. He was kicked out of it; he might have been a poet, but he wasn't one of the gentry.

GC: Burns features in a number of your poems. In what way do you feel connected to him?

WN: Though my surname is originally Irish, it's Irish a long way back. My family has been in Ayrshire since the early sixteenth century. I often stayed on a farm which Burns had visited. Some of my relations lived very near Burns. All farmers, of course. My stepmother's father had a big book of Burns he used to quote from. He wasn't interested much in 'To a Mountain Daisy' but he used to laugh himself stupid at these satirical bits, and read them out loud. That's the first time I really heard them. Of course, he read them in broad Ayrshire. They really struck home. I used to sit in a farm kitchen with a lot of old men — in the days when farms were labour intensive, with lots of incallers and all the rest of it – and the conversation was great to listen to. Even as a boy, I appreciated its saltiness. It was so witty. It used to make me laugh out loud. They did not have TV, they didn't listen to the wireless, they sat round the fire, looking at it and occasionally spitting in it, in the kitchen. They were the salt of the earth, these men, but they were far from being dim or stupid. The modern idea is that if you haven't had any kind of higher education you must be a dimwit. In point of fact a lot of these men would have made professors easily if they had been given the chance. They never were; they were just farm labourers, or ploughman, or cowmen; but they weren't dim; by no means.

GC: That scene you've just painted is something you talk about in 'Ayrshire Farm', the poem which opens your *Selected Poems*. At the end of that poem the man in the family dies, and his wife redecorates the whole place, and you don't feel comfortable with that at all. Is this indicative too of your way of seeing poetry, that you think of it as –

WN: – slightly old-fashioned?

GC: ...no, no, not necessarily old-fashioned. I'm not sure I believe there's an old-fashioned subject matter. I mean that you see poetry as close to the roots, close to the bones of things, not a thing of affectation.

WN: Well it is close to the bones of things. It's the oldest literature there is, in any language. People wrote verse in preference to prose, because verse is memorable. That's the point: it was filled with devices that made it memorable. That, to me, is the great trouble with the modern stuff. It's not memorable. It's as flat as a pancake, and generally undecipherable.

GC: You wrote to me once apropos free verse, and said 'I am also a maker of formal verses'. I was interested in that because it was one of the first occasions on which I came across the idea of poetry as someone making something, as one would make a table or chair.

WN: Poets were called carpenters of verse. The Gaelic name MacIntyre means literally 'son of the joiner', but the joiner being discussed is a carpenter of verse. I don't say that you never found a carpenter in the Highlands who had sons who would be described as the son of the carpenter; what I do mean is that it is much more likely to have been an acronym for a poet than otherwise. The Gaels were very fond of makars. If you made a chair badly it wouldn't last, would fall to bits, and you'd fall off it. If verse isn't well made, it won't stand up, you won't remember it. Now poetry is a different thing; it's something which happens if you're lucky. You don't think, I'm going out this afternoon by the loch to look for some essences; you'd be more likely to write a satirical piece about how you fell in, which is a bit more real. But this is how I see it. I may be an ass. I agree with MacCaig's idea that he never called what he wrote poetry. He always called it verse. It was up to others to give it the name poetry if they found it so. You used to get men who wrote verse which only occasionally was poetry; now you get men writing what is alleged to be poetry but is never verse. That's what's wrong with the whole thing. Over the road there, there's a place called 'Barnboards', and 'Barnboard' looks like an English word. It's nothing to so with Barns or Boards. It's simply 'Bail' na Bard', 'the house that was the maintenance of a poet'. Then there was 'Dervaird', down the road, which means 'the wood of the bard'. This is the trouble with Scotland: not enough people know what the names mean. Dotted everywhere are place-names which are linked to bards. This means that at one time they were men not just of intellectual substance, but prosperous and important citizens. If they wrote satire they wrote it about somebody far away, not about their own chieftain, if they wanted a happy life. One of the local names for instance, MacNellie has nothing to do with Neill, it derives from Mac an Filidh, which means 'the son of the master poet'. A Filidh was a master poet, whereas a bard was just going out and entertaining. He was the man who came on before the big turn, if you like.

GC: We were talking about the feeling for authentic life at the end of your poem 'Ayrshire Farm', and how whenever that had gone you didn't feel you could be comfortable in that farmhouse. What that implies about the writing of verse as you practice it is a search for an authentic utterance, something straight from the heart, unaffected…There are a number of your poems which contain characters who are on the periphery. They are the characters who seem to have that authenticity, are what one could call the truth-tellers. Tell me about your brief lyric 'Demodocus'.

WN: It's a poem against modern pretensions, about business men who regard themselves as terribly important. In comes this man who's not in the least important. This is taken from the *Odyssey* of course. In fact, he is important, because he…he knows more than they do, in a sort of way. Not financially, or in any other social way. Yet he is important because he knows about what makes the human race tick. 'I know that I know more than the men of Athens,' says Socrates, 'because I know at least one thing, that I know nothing.' A very revealing statement. He'd been arguing all his life and had never come to any conclusions, but he knows it. This word 'knowing' is very difficult to explicate. Knowing means more than being able to memorise the formula for solving quadratic equations.

GC: Balefire in some of your English poems is a character who has a truth-telling role, and he's counterpointed by a character called Spondee. Balefire personifies what you might call the Dionysian.

WN: Tom Scott appearing at the poetry reading.

GC: Uncultured as a hedge?

WN: Uncultured only in outward appearance.

GC: You approve of what you could call a 'shaggy knowledge': a culturedness that is mixed with a certain wildness?

WN: I often used to think of Tom Scott in that context. I sometimes met him at poetry readings, when he would say out loud very scathing things about other characters in the offing which definitely wouldn't make him popular. Spondee is the man who is proper and well behaved. He doesn't rock the boat. Balefire is rocking the boat all the time. It seems to him it ought to be rocked. Unwisely, he doesn't care that it's being rocked, that people won't like him any more. He wants them to think about what he says. Of course they don't. And this just makes him more angry.

GC: Have you been a Balefire?

WN: Sometimes.

GC: MacDiarmid said he'd always seen his task as being that of the catfish which animated the torpid inhabitants of the aquarium. Is that the task of your type of poet?

WN: Yes. It's to keep people's eyes on matters that are important. As a Scot, it's important to look at the culture of Scotland, what's under the surface – what remains of it – and to disregard a lot of the bullshit that has grown up, instead, foisted on us by people who should know better. The theme that Scots was never spoken north of the Highland line, for instance, or that Gaelic was never spoken south of it. Absolute nonsense. You can look up that hill there. That farm's called 'Drumskellie', that one's 'Drumlean', the next one over is 'Drumquintin'. Every single name of those is Gaelic. What's more, the men who farm them too have Gaelic names, and they've been here for centuries. I affirm that poets should be learned in the subjects they profess to be interested in. They should know what they're talking about. A poet in Gaeldom, if he was to be a Filidh, had to do a ten year stint. In other words, the equivalent of an MA, a BA and a PhD, before he was let loose on an unsuspecting public.

GC: Would that make him a poet?

WN: It would make him a scholarly versifier. But at least he would know what he was talking about.

GC: You're unique in that you write in Scotland's three languages. What made you decide to learn Gaelic?

WN: Well I wanted to study the poetry.

GC: Your linguistic interest began first as an interest in poetry?

WN: I think it did. I always like the conversation of people rather than reading a book about them. I liked to hear men in the fields speaking expressively in Scots. The people I did hear were farm labourers, and miners who would join them in the fields to earn extra money. They talked intelligently. This is a thing that isn't much realised today. We had fellas galloping about on the slates on the roof who used to be pupils of mine. I remember thinking when they were up there that these fellas knew what to do with cement and bricks. They knew how to put a roof on this place to stop the rain coming in, how to lay felt on it, how to get up ladders and stay up there without falling off. I thought to myself, god, what do you know that these fellas don't? You've been to a university and you don't know half of what these fellas do. I think there's room in the world for the right kind of humility in education. We tend to have a world filled with academic bigheads. Not all of them, but some of them are. Now, for a poet, especially, the first qualification is to become a professor.

GC: No, that's too extreme.

WN: You think that's an exaggeration?

GC: Surely it is. *You*'re not a professor.

WN: I'm fond of quoting that Houseman was fired out of the university without a degree. Actually, he wrote learned essays about Latin because he knew about it, was very keen on it. These essays were so good and so knowledgeable that they had to invite him back and make him a professor at Cambridge. He knew more about Latin than any other man. I'm fond of pointing out that ineffectual scholars are often good poets. Wordsworth, for instance. It's a modern view that you have to be highly educated in order to be a poet. Yet some of the best poetry has been written by those who've been quite mad. Blake, for instance.

GC: How does that square with what you said earlier about poets having to be erudite?

WN: Well, those poets were too learned for their own good perhaps. But at least they knew something. And they were educated to make poems. Although they were sycophants in a way – they had to flatter the chieftains – some of the stuff that dripped over the edges were good.

GC: Your awareness of tradition is obviously not the same as that of lots of other Scottish poets, because of your knowledge of the three tongues of Scotland. How does that modify your view of a Scottish Tradition?

WN: You can't be aware of Scotland unless you know something of the Scottish background. I can walk up to the village and find men who will converse in the Gaelic tongue. I just have to go outside my own door to hear men speaking Scots. And of course like every other Scot I've been brainwashed into learning standard Scottish English. What I'm actually doing is expressing Scotland in the language of Scotland. I'm a Scottish poet. This to me is important. The only other poet I can think of who could use the three languages was George Campbell Hay.

GC: George Campbell Hay is very neglected now, isn't he? Was he an influence?

WN: He shouldn't be neglected. Yes, his poetry was a great influence. He knew all sorts of languages like Arabic, classical Greek, modern Greek. He was an extremely clever man, yet he was in a way, that great thing, a humble man, with his head stuffed. That one small head could carry all he knew! He knew about Scotland. He didn't just claim to know about highland Scotland, but about the whole of Scotland. And he wrote in Scots, Gaelic and English. To do this of course is to court disaster. Critics say things like, he never developed his full potential because it was split up three ways. As if everyone who wrote only English had a mine of concentrated spirituality which always came out as poetry. Nonsense!

GC: A critic wouldn't be talking about a 'mine of spirituality'. He or she would perhaps wonder if writing in the three languages means a poet wouldn't have developed the inwardness with the one language necessary to write well in it.

WN: I'll go along with that. But in order to make that criticism, remember you have to be George Campbell Hay. In other words, you have to know the three languages.

GC: I'm not making that criticism. Has your versatility, linguistically, inhibited critics? Your books often contain, in a sense, three poets, all using a different tongue. Has that versatility made critics defensive, and therefore more likely to ignore you than otherwise?

WN: Something has made them defensive. The amount of critical newsprint accorded to me doesn't amount to more than a few column inches.

GC: Your hardback, *Selected Poems,* was never reviewed in *The Scotsman,* one of Scotland's two major daily broadsheets. That's surprising.

WN: It's par for the course. The way to get noticed in Scotland is not to be a maverick, but to do something in the modern idiom. The whole impression given is that the kind of writing considered important is that which deals with the underprivileged shuffling round the centre of the city in some kind of urban sprawl. It may be accurate but it's hardly entertaining. As far as I'm concerned folk should get out of the urban sprawl as quickly as they can.

GC: Very often they can't do that.

WN: I appreciate that I've been lucky, but I don't think a lot of them really try.

GC: It's always difficult to talk about what others should do. We don't know what's going on in folk's psyches. Your portrait has sometimes been put up among the gallery of poets hanging in Milne's Bar in Edinburgh. A few years ago someone smashed it. Why was that?

WN: I don't know. Better ask the person who smashed it.

GC: Do you know who it was?

WN: No. There are a lot of people in Edinburgh who don't like me very much. I'm not sure why. Perhaps I've done a Balefire on them sometime.

GC: You were very outspoken when in Edinburgh?

WN: Oh yes. Most native speakers of Gaelic were kindness itself in helping me when I was learning to speak the language, but there were one or two exceptions. I had a leading light in Edinburgh, when I won the Bardic Crown at the Mod, say he would rather that anyone won it instead of a bloody lowlander like me. And I said, 'Well, I won it didn't I?', which enraged him even more.

GC: Was he a Highlander?

WN: He was the kind of Highlander who lived in Edinburgh and was never seen in his native airt. He was born in the highlands, but never went there if he could avoid it. And another time there was a well-known Gael who, when I walked into a certain boozer, shouted, 'We don't want any imitation Highlanders in here!' I said, 'I wasn't trying to be an imitation Highlander, I just happen to know your language. I could have spent my time learning German or Russian more profitably, no doubt. I'm perfectly happy about the area I was born in.' He thought I was going to wither, but I just answered back. But that didn't make me very popular. I don't know who did smash this picture, but it could have been someone like that. Particularly if they have some pedestal to stand on. If they're valued in society for some aspect of culture, if you like, like being a critic, or a media buff, or involved in publishing, then you often get this. It has affected me to the extent of having my photograph smashed, not being allowed to hang in The Pantheon in Milne's Bar. It annoys me, of course, but it doesn't worry me one little bit.

GC: It's a sort of accolade, isn't it? It's a mark of the feelings you aroused in some folk, obviously. No doubt as a younger man you said some very unpopular things.

WN: Oh, I didn't go out of my way to give the soft word to people who weren't giving soft words to me. I remember spleen erupting at all sorts of things. If they wanted to bad mouth me, I didn't give the answer that turneth away wrath. When I was younger I gave the answer that made even more wrath. But this was usually with the kind of people I wanted to encourage wrath in. I still get snippets of this from time to time. I know well that some of them have memories like bloody elephants. It's like MacCaig says about Scottish poets. When a Scottish poet comes up and slaps you on the back, make sure he hasn't a dagger in his fist. I suppose it goes on in every poetic society. But if they're jealous of you, it means they're saying that you're better than they are, so that's an accolade too. But I don't live in Edinburgh anymore, so it doesn't make any odds. People round here know I write poetry and they'll tell anybody where I live, but they're not upset by it. Poetry's not the kind of thing they're really into. Maybe I malign them. Maybe they buy my books by the score.

GC: How do you think Scots compares to English for poetry?

WN: Scots is a more fitting language for satire. You can really ding them doun in Scots: it has a sort of Nordic force to it which southern English has lost. Anglo-Saxon and Middle English had that kind of force. But I'm afraid that only mavericks like R S Thomas get home in modern English. That's only because he's writing from a background of Welshness of some kind. But don't get me wrong. I haven't got anything against the English as a people, I'm just saying that modern English has lost the force that it once had. It's an excellent language for almost everything, but it has lost some of its poetic ability to express things.

GC: Surely it depends on who's writing it.

WN: Oh yes. I'm perhaps being cruel about it.

GC: I'm thinking about issue 2 of *The Dark Horse*, in which we did a feature about the word 'irradiate', in a Richard Wilbur poem which was submitted to the *New Yorker* magazine. An editor there wanted this particular word changed, because – at least this was an implication – this was a word which had been debased by modern usage. Wilbur refused to change it. He said that poets, irrespective of whether the advertising men have taken a word and debased it, had to use that word with regard to its original meaning: to reclaim it for poetry.

WN: I do so agree! Poets should recoin old words where they have fallen out of use. Scots words like 'thole', for instance, are sharp and meaningful. One of the things that people who write in Scots are accused of is 'dictionary dredging', which implies that no English poet writing in English ever used a dictionary. I used a word 'flumgummery' in a letter to an editor this morning, which means 'absurd falderals', and I wouldn't be surprised if he changes it. I haven't revived it, I just know it, though I looked it up to make sure. Sure as fate, someone will read it and say that 'as long as Neill uses words like 'flumgummery' he'll never be understood.'

GC: Irrespective of the opinions of critics, a lot of people I think have picked up on the authenticity of what you're doing. I remember giving a copy of *Making Tracks* to a friend of mine, not an assiduous reader of contemporary verse, but with a degree in English, and who's Scottish-Irish. He came back and said, 'This man is one of Scotland's best poets. Why have I never heard of him?'

WN: (laughter) Oh well, you'd better ask the establishment.

GC: I've heard members of the establishment say of you: 'William Neill? He's an *angry* man.'

WN: Do I strike you as being angry?

GC: No. But is there anything wrong with being an angry man?

WN: Oh, nothing at all. Provided you're angry about the right things. Jesus Christ was an angry man. So were the Apostles. Isaiah was an angry man. If you disapprove of anything to a great degree, then you must be an angry man. But I don't go round in a perpetual ferment of rage. I do occasionally boil over, but not all the time. And I think when I'm being satirical it's at a fairly uninflamed level; it's sarcastic if you like, rather than nasty.

GC: Your work is perhaps more appreciated in the US and on the continent than in Scotland.

WN: It's actually been translated into Danish, German and Italian. I can't understand why it's been so difficult to be recognised in Scotland, or even in England, when I'm accepted on the continent; these people are at a linguistic remove, except for Andrea Fabbri in Italy who did a post-graduate course in Aberdeen, and can write letters in Scots. Why should they think it's alright and yet I have so much trouble at home? There is an ambit in which my work is known, but not in the way that would sell books. It doesn't get any great critical acclaim.

GC: Part of the problem about just writing poetry is that folk rarely read poems for their own sake. It's something that Eddie Morgan talks about, in regard to the *Birthday Letters*: that that book will sell huge numbers of copies perhaps as much because people are as interested in Hughes and Plath as in poetry. Hype helps books to sell. We're in a personality culture. But irrespective of their fashionability, lots of your poems stay in place. To paraphrase Seamus Heaney, you can kick them about and they remain unaffected. Take this poem in Scots, 'Hertsaw' [Heart Balm] from your *Selected Poems*:

> Ye're a byornar scunner
> deleerit and rouch,
> stauchran hame et midnicht,
> faa'n doon i the sheuch.
>
> Whit fur ye're no coortin
> wi an ee tae get mairrit
> on the dochter o yon fairm
> wi nae sons tae inherit?
>
> Yon yin thet refuised ye
> has sidled yir harns;
> take saw fir a sair hert:
> kye and weel-biggit barns.
>
> The morn when yer heid stouns
> and dings like a smiddy,
> take tent whit I tellt ye
> and wad muckle Biddy.

WN: That's exactly what the father would say to the son. It's what peasants do think about: the father feeling that this son is wasting his time getting pissed and not doing as his daddy tells him, which he will do in the end. Unless he's a real maverick.

GC: A reader quickly notices you have this tremendous capability in using formal stanzas. Did you have to set yourself consciously to learn these?

WN: I probably absorbed them, more than anything else. I had two very good English teachers at Ayr Academy, Davy Caldwell and Frank Inglis.They taught you what a sonnet was. I bolstered this up with reading too. I like the sonnet form, witty sonnets. And there was one female teacher at Ayr Academy who was red hot on the Border Ballads. 'Sir Patrick Spens', 'Helen of Kirkconnel Lea', 'Binnorie, O Binnorie'. And this stuck with me. I liked it, though I'd never have confessed it. But it had to have a rhythm to it, I didn't like formless stuff. I remember walking home reciting things like 'The Charge of the Light Brigade'. Though I knew that I'd be despised as a lover of Tennyson, I actually liked him. I haven't much time for him maundering on about nature red in tooth and claw, but this was the Victorian thing to do. And other things were good, if murdered by being too often repeated at New Year and similar occasions: 'ring out wild bells to the wild sky'.

GC: When did you start writing?

WN: I wrote my first poem at the age of ten. Rank plagiarism. In one of Blackie's books there was a poem about a crab living on the sea shore. I plagiarised this mightily, and read it, and my father thought I was a second Robert Burns.

GC: It was a rhyming poem, presumably.

WN: Oh yes. Even now, schoolkids all say 'has this one got a rhyme, sir?' I discovered this when I was teaching in Castle Douglas High School. We used these poetry anthologies packed to the brim with formless stuff which didn't produce any reaction. One day I was looking in the cupboard, and all the modern books were gone. All that was left, mouldering in the corner, were the old poetry books that had been read by their fathers. So I got them out, took them in, and we did parts of 'The Deserted Village', and Gray's 'Elegy'. And the following week in the English lesson I said we would do a poem. One girl at the front said, 'Can we no have thon poem that we did last week, aboot the graveyaird?' That's what they wanted to do. I'd been sitting explaining about this poet sitting in Stoke Poges churchyard writing this melancholy poem, and they actually wanted this poem again. 'Why do you like that?' said I; they liked that it was about the great sadness of the graveyard, but the main thing was, 'it has a beat to it, sir, and it rhymes'. This is the memorableness thing again. People want to have memorable verse.

GC: Memorableness isn't such a great virtue alone, though is it? I mean, 'two wee boys sitting on the stair/ one was baldy and one had hair' is memorable. But it's not much more than that!

WN: Yes, it's memorable because it has form, even though it doesn't say very much. I persist in thinking that if verse has lost the quality of memorability, it has lost something very valuable.

GC: So how do you feel about free verse?

WN: I have no inbuilt objections to it. But I agree with Eliot that there's no such thing as free verse. Good free verse is written by someone who knows what a sonnet is.

GC: You've also done narrative verse. I remember pointing out in an editorial that we had our formalists way before the American New Formalists got on the scene, because I would get letters from US poets saying things like, 'I'm really glad to see the New Formalism has reached Scotland' (laughter). One of their big things is narrative. I remember mentioning your very engaging, poem 'The Harnpan' [The Skull]. It fits in with the New Formalist 'program' in America, but it happens to have been written long before New Formalism was heard of. Did you have a model for that poem?

WN: Not really. If I had, it would have been something fantastical like Barham's 'Lord Scroope'. That struck me as a very funny poem. 'The Harnpan' is based on an old Gaelic tale about the man who's walking along with a shinty stick, and he sees something poking out of the ground. He thinks it's a ball, and takes a skelp at it, and it's a skull; in the original tale, the skull told him to take it before the king and he would be well rewarded, because it would speak. He took it to the king, and it refused to say anything, though it talked to the man all the way to the palace. The king said, 'right, you be on parade tomorrow morning, and if that skull doesn't speak to me you'll get your own skull chopped off.' My poem was a variant on that... In the original the man blackmailed the skull in some way to get it to speak – a very Highland thing to do (laughter).

GC: You've often been categorised as a rampant Scottish Nationalist. How do you feel about Nationalism?

WN: It's not widely recognised that the greatest nationalists in Britain are in fact the English. Anybody who doesn't notice this is short on perception. They have dominated every part of Britain, they've made their language supreme – their brand of that language, the language of the English public schools – and they have been cunning enough to spread the fantasy, if you like, that they are not nationalist, everybody else is. The Irish go around shooting people in their frustration, the Scots want to have their own parliament, as they once had. If I am spoken to by an Englishman I feel absolutely no animosity towards him. I mean, Dodo's English. As a matter of fact, I rather like the English. They're quite decent. This is very big of me, to say so. So I don't have any hang-ups in that direction. At the same time I think that the associated kingdoms of

Britain have suffered by being pushed into a corner by the major culture. This irritates me. Especially the bland assumption that everything the bigger culture does is right. You probably know the story about the old woman who was supposed to have been standing outside the parliament when they dismissed for the last time. She said to her cronies, 'when the chiels came oot the parliament hoose and ye thocht they had din wrang, you could caa stanes aboot their lugs, but it's a gey lang throw ti London.' And I think she was right. I'm a nationalist for no other reason than that. Government has to be close to the people so you can go there and pit the heid on them if you disapprove. It doesn't mean that you slavishly agree with everything they've done. I think there should be a parliament in every part of the British Isles. I think the English were stupid to refuse them and I think they'll regret that decision. The heptarchy that once was in England survives in that the north of England is still a different place from the south of England; economically, even linguistically, and certainly culturally. A well known Scottish Nationalist in this area once said to me, 'If the English parliament had been at York there'd have been no need for any talk of nationalism. It would have been central, people would have felt closer to it.' But the current set-up in London, with all these characters going round in red dressing gowns – it's not democratic. These people were never elected. I suppose I must be some kind of socialist in that I want a fair government, and I don't think we'll ever get it with this current arrangement. I don't think that Scotland is a superior place containing superior people. I'll tell you a funny story. There's a wee man runs the village shop. Both his parents were from Lancashire. I often had arguments with the old man, Chippie Wood. His son, Geoff, is a member of the local Burns Club, understands broad Scots perfectly well, and speaks it. He said to me one day: 'Hey Willie , are you for drivin aa the English out of Scotland?' I said, 'Certainly not. If they want to live here, it doesn't matter their origins. I'm quite happy that they live here, and call themselves Scots or not, but no, I don't want to drive the English out of Scotland.' 'Well that's fine then,' he says, 'because I have a nightmare,' he says: 'I can see me openin my mooth in the centre of Carlisle and them caain stanes aboot me'. This man is totally integrated into the culture of his local area. I'm not a Fascist. I don't think all Scots good, all English bad. I don't belong to that faction. But I think if you're not a member of a community which has a governed head then such culture as you have disappears. I like people to have a culture.

GC: Diversity?

WN: Yes. But I despair when they start to fight about it. I despaired about the Irish situation because I knew perfectly well that a lot of it was bogus. The first book of Irish I ever possessed was written by a man called the Reverend William Neilson, who was born in 1870 or thereabouts. Lots of books in Irish were written by Protestants. This modern thing about the great divide is just bullshit. There were lots of Gaelic speaking Protestants. After all, some of them brought the Scottish variety across from Kintyre. It used to irritate me no end when they came out with bogus history to prove their point. I'd say things like, 'Well, Robert Emmet, Wolfe Tone, all that lot were Prods, and there were actually some presbyterians who were agin the Government'. Knowing things like this it used to irritate me when folk spoke the reverse. But I'm like that, you see. It probably annoys people.

GC: How would you best like to have your work – I don't want to say 'remembered', because that sounds too posthumous...

WN: Well, let's be realistic. I'm coming up on 77. I'm going to snuff it within the next five to ten years, if not tomorrow. I've no illusions about that.

GC: Do you have a sense of your own achievement – irrespective of how others will view your writing?

WN: I don't actually, because I've been dinged doun – not by people of your generation, but of my own generation. For instance, when I was left out of *The Best of Scottish Poetry*, I was very bitter about that, because I thought I warranted at least one poem.

GC: Well, these sorts of pubication are ripe for satire, aren't they? Especially when they use the definite article in the title.

WN: Well, books of mine came out around then which didn't sell very well, so I was in a kind of limbo. I felt I hadn't really been accorded any laurels in the poetic sphere, and I relaxed. I stopped being angry about it. I began to accept it. Anyway I had a fairly realistic view of my work. I knew that this wasn't poetry, for the most part, but that it was verse, and that some of it was good verse, and that some of the satirical stuff was better than most. But until the Italians noticed this too my morale had sunk fairly low. Suddenly this young Italian woman had noticed my work, and had liked my satiric vein – vein of satirico, she called it – and felt that was what I was best at. The Italians like my satire, and Iain MacDonald, who's an officer of the Gaelic Books Council likes my Gaelic stuff, and nobody can quarrel with me about my Scots, although people make pooh-pooh noises about it who don't know as much Scots as I do. They often try to catch me out, they think ah cannae speik Scots, it'll no come to ma tongue aw that eithly. It'll come to ma tongue as readily as Standard English. Scots is my native language after all.

GC: Well, there's a difference between quality and fashionableness. You may not be a fashionable poet, but by that token, MacDiarmid wasn't a fashionable poet.

WN: Well, MacDiarmid wrote reviews under a pen name saying how much he admired his own stuff, which I've never had the gall to do. I've been tempted once or twice (laughter).

GC: I'd like you to finish with your masterly sonnet about Burns in the year he died, 'Poet's Walk 1796'.

WN: Certainly:

> Exciseman Burns wannert the kittle toun,
> his wame aw wersh wi drink, his hert wi gaw;
> wha tentit him in this thrawn bit ava?
> Nou nocht tae dae but staucher roun and roun
> frae White Sands tae Midsteeple, up and doun
> the banks o Nith, aye waitin for the caa
> o the Caledonian Muse. The bitch had fled awa
> an widna yield a sang tae a gauger's tune.
>
> Thro grey Dumfries the cauld broon watter gaed,
> droonin the speirit as it smoort the rime
> oot tae a stick's tap on the causey stanes.
>
> Whiles the faur city flittert in his heid.
> As daurk St Michael's bydit for his time
> the smirr o Solway stoundit in his banes.

Glossary

abuin	above	ee	eye
ahint	behind	eidentlie	diligently
atour	across	eith	easy
aye	always	ettle	attempt
bejant	first year student	fankil	tangle
	at a Scottish	fash	fuss
	University	ferlie	wonder
bigg	build	fernie-tickilt	freckled
binna	except	flains	arrows
birk	wood	fleein	blind drunk
birlin	twirling	foondert	destroyed
blate	timid	fremit	strange
blauds	manuscripts	fufft	sulked angrily
braisant	bold	gar	compel
bye	aside	gauger	exiseman
caa	cast	gaw	gall
cadie	bonnet	gey	very
caismeachd	war-march	gin	if
callant	youth	girn	complain
causey stanes	paving	glaur	mud
chiel	fellow	glisk	glance
clashin	gossiping	gowpit	gulped
courie	crouch	gyte	mad
crack	conversation	haet	particle
crannreuch	frost	hap	wrap
cry	call	harn	brain
daurg	toil	hause	neck
dern	conceal	hogget	yearling sheep
dicht	wipe	hotchin	mobbed
dings	rings	howe	hollow
dirk	dagger	howff	pub
dominie	teacher	hoy	convey
dowie	doleful	ilka	each
droukit	soaked	jimp	scarce
duans	verses	kenspeckle	well-known
duine-uasal	gentleman	kirsent	christened
dule	grief	kittle	wicked
dunt	beat	kye	cattle
dwaum	dream	lairstane	tombstone
dyke	wall	lauch	laugh

laverock	lark	skailt	scattered
leid	language	skeilie	skilful
ligg	lie	skep	basket
loun	lad	sleikit	sly
lowe	glow	smirr	drizzle
lowin chaffs	blushing cheeks	smoort	smothered
lowp	leap	sonsie	good natured
lugs	ears	souch	sigh
maun	must	spaewife	fortune teller
mensefu	intelligent	speir	question
mirk	dark	speug	sparrow
mishanter	accident	Spondyls	manipulated
mou	mouth	standard habbie	Scots verse metre
muckle	big	staucher	stagger
muir	moor	stecht	stuffed
mymins	imitations	stieve	firm
mynd	remember	stoun	ache
neb	nose	stoundit	ached
nesh	tender	stowp	flagon
nieve	fist	syne	since
ocht	anything	tacksman	landowner
orra	common	tapsalteerie	upside-down
oxter	armpits	thae	those
pan-loaf	affected speech	thir	these
partans	crabs	thirled	joined
pauchilt	cheating	thole	endure
peelie-wallie	pale	thorter	obstruction
pooch	pocket	thowless	imprudent
preen	pin	thraan	stubborn
quittance	payment	tint	lost
raploch	rough	tozie	tipsy
rauch	rough	ugsome	horrid
raxed	reached	virr	strength
Rigbane	Backbone	wame	stomach
sark	shirt	wersh	sour
sclimm	climb	yeik	itch
screive	write	yelloched	roared
scunner	disgust	yill	ale
seenil	seldom	yirdin	burial
sharrow	bitter	yowder	odour
sheuch	ditch		
siccan	such		

Some other books published by **LUATH** PRESS

'Nothing but Heather!'

Gerry Cambridge

ISBN 0 946487 49 9 PBK £15.00

 Enter the world of Scottish nature – bizarre, brutal, often beautiful, always fascinating – as seen through the lens and poems of Gerry Cambridge, one of Scotland's most distinctive contemporary poets.

On film and in words, Cambridge brings unusual focus to bear on lives as diverse as those of dragonflies, hermit crabs, short-eared owls, and wood anemones. The result is both an instructive look by a naturalist at some of the flora and fauna of Scotland and a poet's aesthetic journey.

This exceptional collection comprises 48 poems matched with 48 captioned photographs. In his introduction Cambridge explores the origins of the project and the approaches to nature taken by other poets, and incorporates a wry account of an unwillingly-sectarian, farm-labouring, bird-obsessed adolescence in rural Ayrshire in the 1970s.

'Keats felt that the beauty of a rainbow was somehow tarnished by knowledge of its properties. Yet the natural world is surely made more, not less, marvellous by awareness of its workings. In the poems that accompany these pictures, I have tried to give an inkling of that. May the marriage of verse and image enlarge the reader's appreciation and, perhaps, insight into the chomping, scurrying, quivering, procreating and dying kingdom, however many miles it be beyond the door.'
GERRY CAMBRIDGE

'a real poet, with a sense of the music of language and the poetry of life...' KATHLEEN RAINE
'one of the most promising and original of modern Scottish poets... a master of form and subtlety.'
GEORGE MACKAY BROWN

Men & Beasts: Wild Men and Tame Animals of Scotland

Poems and Prose by Valerie Gillies

Photographs by Rebecca Marr

ISBN 0 946487 92 8 PBK £15.00

 Come and meet some wild men and tame beasts. Explore the fleeting moment and capture the passing of time in these portrait studies which document a year's journey. Travel across Scotland with poet Valerie Gillies and photographer Rebecca Marr: share their passion for a land where wild men can sometimes be tamed and tame beasts can get really wild.

Among the wild men they find are a gunner in Edinburgh Castle, a Highland shepherd, a ferryman on the River Almond, an eel fisher on Loch Ness, a Borders fencer, and a beekeeper on a Lowland estate.

The beasts portrayed in their own settings include Clydesdale foals, Scottish deerhounds, Highland cattle, blackface sheep, falcons, lurchers, bees, pigs, cashmere goats, hens, cockerels, tame swans and transgenic lambs.

Photograph, poem and reportage - a unique take on Scotland today.

'Goin aroon the Borders wi Valerie an' Rebecca did my reputation the world o good. It's no often they see us wi beautiful talented women, ye ken.' WALTER ELLIOT, fencer and historian
'These poems are rooted in the elemental world.'
ROBERT NYE, reviewing The Chanter's Tune in The Times
'Valerie Gillies is one of the most original voices of the fertile avant-guarde Scottish poetry.' MARCO FAZZINI, l'Arco, Italia
'The work of Valerie Gillies and Rebecca Marr is the result of true collaboration based on insight, empathy and generosity.' JULIE LAWSON, Studies in Photography
'Rebecca Marr's photos never fall into the trap of mere illustration, but rather they show a very individual vision – creative interpretation rather than prosaic document.' ROBIN GILLANDERS, photographer

Half the royalties gained for the sale of theis publication will go to Maggie's Centre for the care of cancer patients.

Poems to be read aloud

Collected and with an introduction by Tom Atkinson

ISBN 0 946487 00 6 PBK £5.00

This personal collection of doggerel and verse ranging from the tear-jerking *Green Eye of the Yellow God* to the rarely printed, bawdy *Eskimo Nell* has a lively cult following. Much borrowed and rarely returned, this is a book for reading aloud in very good company, preferably after a dram or twa. You are guaranteed a warm welcome if you arrive at a gathering with this little volume in your pocket.

'This little book is an attempt to stem the great rushing tide of canned entertainment. A hopeless attempt of course. There is poetry of very high order here, but there is also some fearful doggerel. But that is the way of things. No literary axe is being ground.

Of course some of the items in this book are poetic drivel, if read as poems. But that is not the point. They all spring to life when they are read aloud. It is the combination of the poem with your voice, with all the art and craft you can muster, that produces the finished product and effect you seek.

You don't have to learn the poems. Why clutter up your mind with rubbish? Of course, it is a poorly furnished mind that doesn't carry a fair stock of poetry, but surely the poems to be remembered and savoured in secret, when in love, or ill, or sad, are not the ones you want to share with an audience.

So go ahead, clear your throat and transfix all talkers with a stern eye, then let rip!'
TOM ATKINSON

Blind Harry's Wallace

William Hamilton of Gilbertfield

Introduced by Elspeth King

ISBN 0 946487 43 X HBK £15.00
ISBN 0 946487 33 2 PBK £8.99

The original story of the real braveheart, Sir William Wallace. Racy, blood on every page, violently anglophobic, grossly embellished, vulgar and disgusting, clumsy and stilted, a literary failure, a great epic. Whatever the verdict on BLIND HARRY, this is the book which has done more than any other to frame the notion of Scotland's national identity. Despite its numerous 'historical inaccuracies', it remains the principal source for what we now know about the life of Wallace.

The novel and film *Braveheart* were based on the 1722 Hamilton edition of this epic poem. Burns, Wordsworth, Byron and others were greatly influenced by this version 'wherein the old obsolete words are rendered more intelligible', which is said to be the book, next to the Bible, most commonly found in Scottish households in the eighteenth century. Burns even admits to having 'borrowed... a couplet worthy of Homer' directly from Hamilton's version of BLIND HARRY to include in 'Scots wha hae'.

Elspeth King, in her introduction to this, the first accessible edition of BLIND HARRY in verse form since 1859, draws parallels between the situation in Scotland at the time of Wallace and that in Bosnia and Chechnya in the 1990s. Seven hundred years to the day after the Battle of Stirling Bridge, the 'Settled Will of the Scottish People' was expressed in the devolution referendum of 11 September 1997. She describes this as a landmark opportunity for mature reflection on how the nation has been shaped, and sees BLIND HARRY'S WALLACE as an essential and compelling text for this purpose.

'A true bard of the people'.
TOM SCOTT, THE PENGUIN BOOK OF SCOTTISH VERSE, on Blind Harry.

'A more inventive writer than Shakespeare'.
RANDALL WALLACE

'The story of Wallace poured a Scottish prejudice in my veins which will boil along until the floodgates of life shut in eternal rest'.
ROBERT BURNS

'Hamilton's couplets are not the best poetry you will ever read, but they rattle along at a fair pace. In re-issuing this work, the publishers have re-opened the spring from which most of our conceptions of the Wallace legend come'.
SCOTLAND ON SUNDAY

'The return of Blind Harry's Wallace, a man who makes Mel look like a wimp'.
THE SCOTSMAN

On the Trail of Robert Burns

John Cairney

ISBN 0 946487 51 0   PBK   £7.99

Is there anything new to say about Robert Burns?

John Cairney says it's time to trash Burns the Brand and come on the trail of the real Robert Burns. He is the best of travelling companions on this convivial, entertaining journey to the heart of the Burns story.

Internationally known as 'the face of Robert Burns', John Cairney believes that the traditional Burns tourist trail urgently needs to find a new direction. In an acting career spanning forty years he has often lived and breathed Robert Burns on stage. *On the Trail of Robert Burns* shows just how well he can get under the skin of a character. This fascinating journey around Scotland is a rediscovery of Scotland's national bard as a flesh and blood genius.

On the Trail of Robert Burns outlines five tours, mainly in Scotland. Key sites include:

Alloway - Burns' birthplace. 'Tam O' Shanter' draws on the witch-stories about Alloway Kirk first heard by Burns in his childhood.
Mossgiel - between 1784 and 1786 in a phenomenal burst of creativity Burns wrote some of his most memorable poems including 'Holy Willie's Prayer' and 'To a Mouse.'
Kilmarnock - the famous Kilmarnock edition of *Poems Chiefly in the Scottish Dialect* published in 1786.
Edinburgh - fame and Clarinda (among others) embraced him.
Dumfries - Burns died at the age of 37. The trail ends at the Burns mausoleum in St Michael's churchyard.

'For me an aim I never fash
I rhyme for fun'.
ROBERT BURNS

'My love affair on stage with Burns started in London in 1959. It was consumated on stage at the Traverse Theatre in Edinburgh in 1965 and has continued happily ever since'.
JOHN CAIRNEY

'The trail is expertly, touchingly and amusingly followed'. THE HERALD

On the Trail of Robert Service

GW Lockhart

ISBN 0 946487 24 3   PBK   £7.99

Robert Service is famed world-wide for his eye-witness verse-pictures of the Klondike goldrush. As a war poet, his work outsold Owen and Sassoon, and he went on to become the world's first million selling poet. In search of adventure

and new experiences, he emigrated from Scotland to Canada in 1890 where he was caught up in the aftermath of the raging gold fever. His vivid dramatic verse bring to life the wild, larger than life characters of the gold rush Yukon, their bar-room brawls, their lust for gold, their trigger-happy gambles with life and love. 'The Shooting of Dan McGrew' is perhaps his most famous poem:

A bunch of the boys were whooping it up in the Malamute saloon;
The kid that handles the music box was hitting a ragtime tune;
Back of the bar in a solo game, sat Dangerous Dan McGrew,
And watching his luck was his light o'love, the lady that's known as Lou.

His storytelling powers have brought Robert Service enduring fame, particularly in North America and Scotland where he is something of a cult figure.

Starting in Scotland, *On the Trail of Robert Service* follows Service as he wanders through British Columbia, Oregon, California, Mexico, Cuba, Tahiti, Russia, Turkey and the Balkans, finally 'settling' in France.

This revised edition includes an expanded selection of illustrations of scenes from the Klondike as well as several photographs from the family of Robert Service on his travels around the world.

Wallace Lockhart, an expert on Scottish traditional folk music and dance, is the author of *Highland Balls & Village Halls* and *Fiddles & Folk*. His relish for a well-told tale in popular vernacular led him to fall in love with the verse of Robert Service and write his biography.

'A fitting tribute to a remarkable man - a bank clerk who wanted to become a cowboy. It is hard to imagine a bank clerk writing such lines as:
A bunch of boys were whooping it up...
The income from his writing actually exceeded his bank salary by a factor of five and he resigned to pursue a full time writing career.' Charles Munn,
THE SCOTTISH BANKER

'Robert Service claimed he wrote for those who wouldnit be seen dead reading poetry. His was an almost unbelievably mobile life... Lockhart hangs on breathlessly, enthusiastically unearthing clues to the poet's life.' Ruth Thomas,
SCOTTISH BOOK COLLECTOR

'This enthralling biography will delight Service lovers in both the Old World and the New.'
Marilyn Wright,
SCOTS INDEPENDENT

But n Ben A-Go-Go

Matthew Fitt

ISBN 0 946487 82 0   HBK   £10.99

The year is 2090. Global flooding has left most of Scotland under water. The descendants of those who survived God's Flood live in a community of floating island parishes, known collectively as Port.

Port's citizens live in mortal fear of Senga, a supervirus whose victims are kept in a giant hospital warehouse in sealed capsules called Kists.

Paolo Broon is a low-ranking cyberjanny. His life-partner, Nadia, lies forgotten and alone in Omega Kist 624 in the Rigo Imbeki Medical Center. When he receives an unexpected message from his radge criminal father to meet him at But n Ben A-Go-Go, Paolo's life is changed forever.

He must traverse VINE, Port and the Drylands and deal with rebel American tourists and crabbit Dundonian microchips to discover the truth about his family's past in order to free Nadia from the sair grip of the merciless Senga.

Set in a distinctly unbonnie future-Scotland, the novel's dangerous atmosphere and psychologically-malkied characters weave a tale that both chills and intrigues. In *But n Ben A-Go-Go* Matthew Fitt takes the allegedly dead language of Scots and energises it with a narrative that crackles and fizzes with life.

'After an initial shock, readers of this sprightly and imaginative tale will begin to relish its verbal impetus, where a standard Lallans, laced with bits of Dundonian and Aberdonian, is stretched and skelped to meet the demands of cyberjannies and virtual hoorhooses.

Eurobawbees, rooburgers, mutant kelpies, and titanic blooters from supertyphoons make sure that the Scottish peninsula is no more parochial than its language. I recommend an entertaining and ground-breaking book.'
EDWIN MORGAN

'Matthew Fitt's instinctive use of Scots is spellbinding. This is an assured novel of real inventiveness. Be prepared to boldly go...'
ELLIE McDONALD

'Easier to read than Shakespeare – wice the fun.'
DES DILLON

Red Sky at Night

John Barrington

ISBN 0 946487 60 X   PBK   £8.99

'I read John Barrington's book with growing delight. This working shepherd writes beautifully about his animals, about the wildlife, trees and flowers which surround him at all times, and he paints an unforgettable picture of his glorious corner of Western Scotland. It is a lovely story of a rather wonderful life'.
JAMES HERRIOT

John Barrington is a shepherd to over 750 Blackface ewes who graze 2,000 acres of some of Britain's most beautiful hills overlooking the deep dark water of Loch Katrine in Perthshire. The yearly round of lambing, dipping, shearing and the sales is marvellously interwoven into the story of the glen, of Rob Roy in whose house John now lives, of curling when the ice is thick enough, and of sheep dog trials in the summer. Whether up to the hills or along the glen, John knows the haunts of the local wildlife: the wily hill fox, the grunting badger, the herds of red deer, and the shrews, voles and insects which scurry underfoot. He sets his seasonal clock by the passage of birds on the loch, and jealously guards over the golden eagle's eyrie in the hills. Paul Armstrong's sensitive illustrations are the perfect accompaniment to the evocative text.

'Mr Barrington is a great pleasure to read. One learns more things about the countryside from this account of one year than from a decade of The Archers'.
THE DAILY TELEGRAPH

'Powerful and evocative... a book which brings vividly to life the landscape, the wildlife, the farm animals and the people who inhabit John's vista. He makes it easy for the reader to fall in love with both his surrounds and his commune with nature'.
THE SCOTTISH FIELD

'An excellent and informative book.... not only an account of a shepherd's year but also the diary of a naturalist. Little escapes Barrington's enquiring eye and, besides the life cycle of a sheep, he also gives those of every bird, beast, insect and plant that crosses his path, mixing their histories with descriptions of the geography, local history and folklore of his surroundings'. TLS

'The family life at Glengyle is wholesome, appealing and not without a touch of the Good Life. Many will envy Mr Barrington his fastness home as they cruise up Loch Katrine on the tourist steamer'.
THE FIELD

ON THE TRAIL OF

On the Trail of Mary Queen of Scots
J. Keith Cheetham
ISBN 0 946487 50 2 PBK £7.99

On the Trail of William Wallace
David R. Ross
ISBN 0 946487 47 2 PBK £7.99

On the Trail of Bonnie Prince Charlie
David R. Ross
ISBN 0 946487 68 5 PBK £7.99

On the Trail of Queen Victoria in the Highlands
Ian R. Mitchell
ISBN 0 946487 79 0 PBK £7.99

On the Trail of Robert the Bruce
David R. Ross
ISBN 0 946487 52 9 PBK £7.99

LUATH GUIDES TO SCOTLAND

Mull and Iona: Highways and Byways
Peter Macnab
ISBN 0 946487 58 8 PBK £4.95

SouthWest Scotland
Tom Atkinson
ISBN 0 946487 04 9 PBK £4.95

The West Highlands: The Lonely Lands
Tom Atkinson
ISBN 0 946487 56 1 PBK £4.95

The Northern Highlands: The Empty Lands
Tom Atkinson
ISBN 0 946487 55 3 PBK £4.95

The North West Highlands: Roads to the Isles
Tom Atkinson
ISBN 0 946487 54 5 PBK £4.95

WALK WITH LUATH

Mountain Days & Bothy Nights
Dave Brown and Ian Mitchell
ISBN 0 946487 15 4 PBK £7.50

The Joy of Hillwalking
Ralph Storer
ISBN 0 946487 28 6 PBK £7.50

Scotland's Mountains before the Mountaineers
Ian Mitchell
ISBN 0 946487 39 1 PBK £9.99

LUATH WALKING GUIDES

Walks in the Cairngorms
Ernest Cross
ISBN 0 946487 09 X PBK £4.95

Short Walks in the Cairngorms
Ernest Cross
ISBN 0 946487 23 5 PBK £4.95

NEW SCOTLAND

Some Assembly Required: behind the scenes at the rebirth of the Scottish Parliament
Andy Wightman
ISBN 0 946487 84 7 PBK £7.99

Scotland - Land and Power the agenda for land reform
Andy Wightman
ISBN 0 946487 70 7 PBK £5.00

Old Scotland New Scotland
Jeff Fallow
ISBN 0 946487 40 5 PBK £6.99

Notes from the North Incorporating a Brief History of the Scots and the English
Emma Wood
ISBN 0 946487 46 4 PBK £8.99

HISTORY

Reportage Scotland: History in the Making
Louise Yeoman
ISBN 0 946487 61 8 PBK £9.99

Edinburgh's Historic Mile
Duncan Priddle
ISBN 0 946487 97 9 PBK £2.99

SOCIAL HISTORY

Shale Voices
Alistair Findlay
foreword by Tam Dalyell MP
ISBN 0 946487 63 4 PBK £10.99
ISBN 0 946487 78 2 HBK £17.99

Crofting Years
Francis Thompson
ISBN 0 946487 06 5 PBK £6.95

A Word for Scotland
Jack Campbell
foreword by Magnus Magnusson
ISBN 0 946487 48 0 PBK £12.99

BIOGRAPHY

Tobermory Teuchter: A first-hand account of life on Mull in the early years of the 20th century
Peter Macnab
ISBN 0 946487 41 3 PBK £7.99

The Last Lighthouse
Sharma Kraustopf
ISBN 0 946487 96 0 PBK £7.99

Bare Feet and Tackety Boots
Archie Cameron
ISBN 0 946487 17 0 PBK £7.95

Come Dungeons Dark
John Taylor Caldwell
ISBN 0 946487 19 7 PBK £6.95

FOLKLORE

Scotland: Myth Legend & Folklore
Stuart McHardy
ISBN 0 946487 69 3 PBK £7.99

The Supernatural Highlands
Francis Thompson
ISBN 0 946487 31 6 PBK £8.99

Tall Tales from an Island
Peter Macnab
ISBN 0 946487 07 3 PBK £8.99

Tales from the North Coast
Alan Temperley
ISBN 0 946487 18 9 PBK £8.99

MUSIC AND DANCE

Highland Balls and Village Halls
GW Lockhart
ISBN 0 946487 12 X PBK £6.95

Fiddles & Folk: A celebration of the re-emergence of Scotland's musical heritage
GW Lockhart
ISBN 0 946487 38 3 PBK £7.95

FICTION

Grave Robbers
Robin Mitchell
ISBN 0 946487 72 3 PBK £7.99

The Bannockburn Years
William Scott
ISBN 0 946487 34 0 PBK £7.95

The Great Melnikov
Hugh MacLachlan
ISBN 0 946487 42 1 PBK £7.95

POETRY

The Luath Burns Companion
John Cairney
ISBN 1 84282 000 1 PBK £10.00

FOOD AND DRINK

Edinburgh & Leith Pub Guide
Stuart McHardy
ISBN 0 946487 80 4 PBK £4.99

SPORT

Over the Top with the Tartan Army (Active Service 1992-97)
Andrew McArthur
ISBN 0 946487 45 6 PBK £7.99

Ski & Snowboard Scotland
Hilary Parke
ISBN 0 946487 35 9 PBK £6.99

Pilgrims in the Rough: St Andrews beyond the 19th hole
Michael Tobart
ISBN 0 946487 74 X PBK £7.99

CARTOONS

Broomie Law
Cinders McLeod
ISBN 0 946487 99 5 PBK £4.00

Luath Press Limited
committed to publishing well written books worth reading

LUATH PRESS takes its name from Robert Burns, whose little collie Luath (*Gael.*, swift or nimble) tripped up Jean Armour at a wedding and gave him the chance to speak to the woman who was to be his wife and the abiding love of his life. Burns called one of *The Twa Dogs* Luath after Cuchullin's hunting dog in *Ossian's Fingal*. Luath Press grew up in the heart of Burns country, and now resides a few steps up the road from Burns' first lodgings in Edinburgh's Royal Mile.
Luath offers you distinctive writing with a hint of unexpected pleasures.

Most UK and US bookshops either carry our books in stock or can order them for you. To order direct from us, please send a £sterling cheque, postal order, international money order or your credit card details (number, address of cardholder and expiry date) to us at the address below. Please add post and packing as follows: UK – £1.00 per delivery address; overseas surface mail – £2.50 per delivery address; overseas airmail – £3.50 for the first book to each delivery address, plus £1.00 for each additional book by airmail to the same address. If your order is a gift, we will happily enclose your card or message at no extra charge.

Luath Press Limited
543/2 Castlehill
The Royal Mile
Edinburgh EH1 2ND
Scotland
Telephone: 0131 225 4326 (24 hours)
Fax: 0131 225 4324
email: gavin.macdougall@luath.co.uk
Website: www.luath.co.uk